Chatbots in Customer Experience

Application and Opportunities
in E-Commerce

Bibliografische Information der Deutschen Nationalbibliothek:

Die Deutsche Nationalbibliothek verzeichnet diese Publikation in der Deutschen Nationalbibliografie; detaillierte bibliografische Daten sind im Internet über http://dnb.d-nb.de abrufbar.

Impressum:

Copyright © Studylab 2019

Ein Imprint der Open Publishing GmbH, München

Druck und Bindung: Books on Demand GmbH, Norderstedt, Germany

Coverbild: Open Publishing GmbH | Freepik.com | Flaticon.com | ei8htz

Table of Content

List of Figures IV

1 Introduction 1
    1.1 Status Quo and Motivation 1
    1.2 Research Questions and Goals 2
    1.3 Structure 2

2 Theoretical Framework 4
    2.1 Marketing Communications 4
    2.2 Customer Relationship Management 9
    2.3 Chatbots 14

3 Chatbots in E-Commerce 21
    3.1 Implementation throughout the Customer Journey 21
    3.2 Opportunities 30

4 Practical Use Case Analysis and Implementation 37
    4.1 Collection and Selection of Use Cases 37
    4.2 Requirements 37
    4.3 Implementation 42
    4.4 Evaluation 47

5 Conclusion 49

Works Cited 51

List of Figures

Figure 1: Lego's Facebook Messenger Chatbot 23

Figure 2: Argomall's Facebook Messenger Chatbot 24

Figure 3: 1-800-Flowers.com Facebook Messenger Chatbot 27

Figure 4: Otto.de Onlineshop Chatbot "Clara" 30

Figure 5: Trends in usage behavior – Fittkau & Maass Consulting 33

Figure 6: FlowXO 'New Message' 43

Figure 7: FlowXO 'Ask a Question' 44

Figure 8: FlowXO 'Send a Message' 45

Figure 9: FlowXO 'Filter' 46

Figure 10: FlowXO 'Test Console' 47

1 Introduction

This chapter describes the current status quo of the field and the scope of this study. The underlying research questions are used to define the objectives of the study, followed by a discussion of the structure of the thesis.

1.1 Status Quo and Motivation

Customer service within the mail order sector has changed greatly in recent years. E-commerce has developed along with the expansion of the Internet. The increasing digitalization of society, the impact this has had on everyday life and the growing demands and needs of customers pose a new challenge to the economy and especially to e-commerce companies. The important role of digitalization in the form of, for example, constant and real-time connectivity with the Internet as well as the progressive networking of various devices and everyday objects have a major impact on customers' behaviour and expectations. To meet customer demands, companies have established further contact channels so that a comprehensive range of services can be ensured. In addition to competing over who has the best product, companies now compete over who has the best service to differentiate themselves. As such, service is becoming an increasingly important success factor for companies. Companies aim to reduce the cost of customer service without reducing its quality. For this reason, robots will probably take over some tasks in everyday life as well as in professional life in the future. These robots will be able to interact and communicate with people. Through the World Wide Web, people have the opportunity to submit their searches anytime and anywhere. The visitor wants to find the desired information as directly and quickly as possible. Customers expect a comprehensive range of services on many different communication channels and want to self-determine which channel they use for their request. At this point of time, the use of chatbots is optimal to open another contact for customers.[1] The chatbots can assume the function of a human and provide the visitor with competent assistance in finding information.[2]

---

[1] www.ey.com, 28.02.2018
[2] news.chrunchbase.com, 28.02.2018

1.2 Research Questions and Goals

As mentioned above, chatbots can be used in online marketing and customer service. Rather than picking up the phone or sending an e-mail, customers' questions about a product or service can be answered at any time by using chatbots. In the future, people will increasingly come into contact with chatbots, which will result in a change in dialogue and service between the company and its customers. Studying the literature on the topics shows that little is known about how and where chatbots can be used in e-commerce and what benefits they bring. The present work focuses mainly on the Business-to-Consumer (B2C) area, which aims at long-term customer loyalty and satisfaction. Due to artificial intelligence being such a broad subject area, only written interaction between humans and chatbots is discussed. Physical robots or other artificial intelligence are not considered here, nor are the detailed technical functions and structure of a chatbot or its programming explained. [3]

The goal of this thesis is to determine and evaluate the use of chatbots in customer service and online marketing by asking the following questions:

- Where can chatbots be used in customer management and online marketing?
- How does using chatbots in customer service and marketing affect a specific customer journey?
- What are the benefits of using chatbots for both customers and the company?
- What methods and requirements should be considered when using chatbots?

1.3 Structure

A brief overview of the topic is followed by a discussion of the theoretical framework in chapter 2. This section includes an introduction to marketing management in general and a classification into direct marketing, online marketing and social media marketing. Customer relationship management is introduced and the customer experience and customer journey are explained. Furthermore, the definition of chatbots is discussed in detail. Finally, the conceptual architecture is discussed

---

[3] Cf. Damodaran, X. (2011), pp. 44-47

and conversational interfaces are shown. In chapter 3, chatbots are analyzed and explained theoretically, based on their use in e-commerce throughout the customer journey. After this, the opportunities and benefits of chatbots from the corporate and customer perspective are discussed. Next, chapter 4 demonstrates and analyses different use cases. In addition to analytical methods, the requirements for implementing a chatbot are investigated. The chapter also explains possible approaches to the collection and selection of use cases. This is followed by introducing the systematization used to capture requirements, select systems and implement chatbots. Key metrics for the evaluation of chatbots are also described. Chapter 5 evaluates the results, and the thesis concludes with a look forward to identify interesting future research questions and provide an assessment of the use of chatbots.

2 Theoretical Framework

2.1 Marketing Communications

Marketing communications is an area of operative measures that is a part of the classic marketing mix. The term 'marketing mix' is based on McCarthy's classic four P's (product, price, place, and promotion) and describes the combination of marketing communication measures used by a company.[4] Further areas of operative marketing measures are product policy, contracting policy and distribution policy.

Marketing instruments are used for market cultivation.[5] Various instruments are available within marketing communications: communication instruments are typically divided into the sub-areas of advertising, sales promotion, public relations and personal sales.[6] In addition, there are modern instruments which generally include direct marketing, sponsoring, event marketing, product placement and online marketing.[7] Social media marketing can also be included under online marketing.[8]

All marketing communication measures aim to ensure that relevant market participants are sufficiently aware of the range of services on offer, develop an interest in them, feel addressed rationally and emotionally, and buy the product or service. Marketing communications thus has the task of informing potential consumers, influencing them in a targeted manner and overcoming sales resistance.[9] This involves strategic planning of the design, implementation, allocation and control of communication measures. In marketing communications, it is not the factual level that is decisive, but the target person's perception of it, i.e., an emotional meta-level that superimposes the rational, factual level.[10]

Marketing communications can be used to create unique selling propositions. In saturated, strongly segmented markets that are occupied by many suppliers with substitutable products, product-related, unique features that are relevant for the

---

[4] Cf. Runia, P., Wahl, F., Geyer, O., Thewißen, C. (2015), pp. 157-159
[5] Cf. Dahlén, M., Lange, F., & Smith, T. (2010), p. 282
[6] Cf. Runia, P., Wahl, F., Geyer, O., Thewißen, C. (2015), p. 274
[7] Cf. Runia, P., Wahl, F., Geyer, O., Thewißen, C. (2015), pp. 301-328
[8] Cf. Esch, F.-R., Herrmann, A., Sattler, H. (2017), p. 162
[9] Cf. Fill, C. (2001), p. 23
[10] Cf. Kotler, P., Bliemel, F., Keller, K. L. (2017), p. 67

target group are hardly to be found.[11] These kinds of Unique Selling Propositions (USP) are increasingly being replaced by a unique position oriented towards marketing communications, which is referred to as the Unique Communication Proposition (UCP). The UCP concentrates on a unique positioning generated by an advertising service. A substitutable product can be combined with an unmistakable experience profile in the perception of the target group by means of marketing communication instruments. The prerequisite is that the experience profile is relevant for the target group, valid in the long term and not already occupied by competition.[12]

In sum, marketing communications comprises the design of information regarding a company and its products, addressed to a market with the aim of serving the expectations, attitudes and demand of current and potential customers.[13]

Regular exposure to a brand increases the probability that it will be taken into account when making a purchase decision. This requires a clear positioning of the brand, which in turn can be achieved through a clearly focused communications strategy.[14]

2.1.1 Direct Marketing

'Dialogue marketing' is often used synonymously with the term 'direct marketing'. The conceptual definitions are very broad, and therefore a definition of the term and a short summary seem necessary.

Holland has defined dialogue marketing as the establishment of interactive communication with the target person. A company's message is oriented to elicit a reaction. This reaction is recorded, stored and evaluated for the following message. A dialogue takes place.[15] Andreas Mann has conceptualized a special, interaction-related form of customer orientation and referred to three essential characteristics:[16]- Interaction: A mutual exchange of information within a two-way communication link, whereby each participant can assume the role of communicator as well as the role of communicant. - Orientation towards understanding and

---

[11] Cf. Blythe, J. (2012), p. 250
[12] Cf. Runia, P., Wahl, F., Geyer, O., Thewißen, C. (2015), pp. 258-260
[13] Cf. Meffert, H., Burmann, C., Kirchgeorg, M. (2015), p. 437.
[14] Cf. Runia, P., Wahl, F., Geyer, O., Thewißen, C. (2015), pp. 262-264
[15] Cf. Holland, H. (2016), pp. 10-12
[16] Cf. Krafft, M. [ed.], & Mann, A. (2007), pp. 3-27

understanding: A communication without prejudice, in which the dialogue initiator takes the interests of the dialogue participants into account and a mutual reconciliation of interests is strived for. - Pursuit of special (marketing) goals: These are set so that the dialogue with various stakeholder groups delivers a corporate policy benefit for a company.

Direct marketing means the use of consumer-direct channels to reach and deliver goods and services to customers without middlemen. Today, many direct marketers use direct marketing to build a long-term relationship with the customer.[17] Bruhn has described direct marketing as a summary of all communication measures aiming to establish direct contact with the addressee and initiating a direct dialogue through a targeted individual approach or aiming to lay the foundation for a dialogue at a second level through an indirect approach in order to achieve the company's communications goals.[18] Dialogue marketing has been seen as a further development of traditional direct marketing or as modern direct marketing.[19]

In principle, dialogue marketing is aligned to a genuine dialogue and stresses the reciprocity of the relationship between customers and enterprises more strongly.[20] In contrast, direct marketing leads to only illusory dialogues. More and more companies are incorporating direct marketing into their marketing concepts. The purpose of using direct marketing activities is, among other things, to have direct communications with the customer. The enterprise tries to seize the needs of the customer and to deal with them accordingly.[21] Thanks to an individual dialogue with the target customer, the marketer achieves cost savings due to small losses as well as a higher efficiency of its marketing actions.[22] Consumers can be addressed with the help of direct marketing at the correct time, and direct advertising measures also accomplish a higher reading rate due to having an interested

---

[17] Cf. Kotler, P., Bliemel, F., Keller, K. L. (2017), p. 620
[18] Cf. Bruhn, M. (2016), pp. 229-231
[19] Cf. Dallmer, H. (2002), pp. 8-10
[20] Cf. Stone, B., Jacobs, R. (2001), pp. 11-12
[21] Cf. Chaffey, D. (2001), p. 338.
[22] Cf. Holland, H. (2016), p. 87

target group.[23] The Internet strengthens this effect further and this results in benefits for enterprises in the long run.

2.1.2 Online Marketing

Online marketing is a special type of direct marketing, i.e., a type of interactive alignment of marketing instruments through the use of networked information systems such as the Internet.[24] The Internet and online services have opened up new communication channels for marketing. The advantages of online marketing for the customer are uncomplicated communication, the possibility of simple information comparison and the relative unobtrusiveness of the medium. The marketer benefits from online marketing because it is possible to make short-term market and price adjustments, establish customer relationships via the Internet and monitor the success of the online offerings. An online presence can occur in the form of an online office, online advertising, e-mail or through open communication groups.[25] Online marketing thus offers a variety of opportunities for dialogue. In addition, products and services can be ordered online (e.g., from online shops) and further information can be requested by e-mail.

A close look at all online marketing channels reveals two basic strategies. On the one hand, advertising measures can be related to brand marketing.[26] In this case, an attempt is made to increase awareness of a brand, a company or a certain product with the help of broad distribution of advertising media as well as with a widespread acceptance of high costs and wastage. On the other hand, so-called performance marketing uses advertising measures specifically to trigger a measurable reaction from the advertising message's recipients, who are defined as the target of the advertising campaign. The success of these advertising measures is measured after the end of the campaign or, increasingly, in real time, using defined key performance indicators; thus, this approach creates a space for permanent optimization possibilities.[27]

---

[23] Cf. Kotler, P. (2013), p. 547
[24] Cf. Bruhn, M. (2016), p. 413
[25] Cf. Kotler, P., Bliemel, F., Keller, K. L. (2017), p. 1128
[26] Cf. Fill, C., Turnbull, S. (2016), pp. 358-359
[27] Cf. Kamps, I., Schetter, D. (2018), p. 60

2.1.3 Social Media Marketing

'Social media' means the exchange of information, experiences and perspectives through community websites. Examples of social media are blogs, Internet forums, message boards, image and video portals, user-generated websites, wikis and podcasts.[28] The social web is the part of the Internet that deals with social structures and interactions but not with technical backgrounds and program architectures.[29]

Social media marketing comprises strategies and measures to successfully position companies on the social web. It is about making the social (the community) usable through its media (communication and tools) to market something to an audience.[30] When people go online, they spend most of their time on activities on social media. This fact also makes it possible for companies to become active on the Social Web, where they can show their presence to potential customers and exchange ideas with them.

If social media is to be used for marketing purposes, the goal must always be to address potentially attractive customers. Given the wealth of possibilities offered by the German social media landscape, it can be challenging to select a channel on which to create a profile.[31] Social networks offer users the opportunity to connect and exchange information with other participants. These can be acquaintances from the offline world or users with similar interests, views and hobbies. The networks are based on profiles which can be individually adapted and linked to other profiles.[32] Well-known social networks include Facebook, YouTube, Twitter, Instagram, Xing and Snapchat. Companies can also use social networks. On many networks, there are separate pages for commercial members where companies can share news about the company or other information. Interested parties and customers can react to the publications, for example by classifying them as interesting or commenting directly on them.[33] Social networks are frequently used for marketing purposes for a reason: social networks – especially Facebook – achieve a very high rate of reach on the Internet. The information that users reveal about

---

[28] Cf. Weinberg, T. (2015), p. 2
[29] Cf. Ebersbach, A., Glaser, M., & Heigl, R.. (2016), p. 33
[30] Cf. Weinberg, T. (2015), p. 16
[31] Cf. Scott, D. M. (2014), p. 311
[32] Cf. Weinberg, T. (2015), p. 169
[33] Cf. Gabriel, R., Röhrs, H. (2017), p. 18

themselves on their profiles can be used relatively easily to gain insights into the relevant target group and its social environment.[34] New targets with relevant interests are easy to locate and contact. By having a personal and credible presence on social networks, companies have the opportunity to gain or strengthen the trust of users. In this way, companies can tap new target groups and markets that are difficult or impossible to reach by conventional means.[35] Such a presence on the Internet can have a negative effect if it contradicts the rules of social interaction, for example if positive user comments are falsified by the company. Even a presence that is not maintained or whose contents are strongly influenced by advertising lead to negative reactions on the user side and can cause a loss of reputation.[36]

Connecting social networks to online shops is equally feasible as the integration of Facebook plug-ins into the providers' own shop; however, this type of distribution (called social commerce) has played a subordinate role so far.

2.2 Customer Relationship Management

The perception of customer needs and the corresponding reaction to them form the basis of the economic success of companies. This observation is based on the realization that long-term customer relationships have a considerable influence on the realization of corporate goals. In recent years, two developments have had a significant influence on the process of customer relationship management (CRM).

The first development is the transition from transaction marketing to relationship marketing, which meant the end of a focus on individual transactions and propagated a broader view of the customer relationship.[37] Secondly, the shift from an industrial society to an information society or knowledge management enabled rapid development especially in the field of information technology, and as a result applications and process changes produced more diverse and effective marketing measures.[38] An increased intensity of competition and technological change are major reasons for this development.[39] In a scholarly context, it has been

---

[34] Cf. Ceyp, M., Scupin, J. (2013), p. 179
[35] Cf. Koch, M., Richter, A. (2009), pp. 56-59
[36] Cf. Heymann-Reder, D. (2011), p. 29
[37] Cf. Mengue Nkoa, C. (2006), p. 34
[38] Cf. Wirtz, Bernd W. (2018), p. 6
[39] Cf. Rajola, F. (2003), p. 34

established that a focus on individual transactions and the use of classical marketing instruments no longer constitute the most efficient form of a transaction. Accordingly, the consideration and evaluation of business relationships has become more comprehensive and inclusive of all of their facets.[40] Homburg and Bruhn have defined customer relationship management as the systematic analysis, planning, implementation and monitoring of all measures aimed at the current customer base with the aim of ensuring that these customers maintain or intensify their business relationship in the future.[41]

A basic assumption of customer relationship management is basically to maximize customer orientation.[42] The aim is to build and strengthen sustainable relationships with profitable customers in order to bind loyal customers to the company in the long term. In contrast to transaction marketing, the short-term pursuit of profit is not the focus of entrepreneurial activity. The focus is on tapping the entire volume of customer value that can be realized over the entire customer lifecycle.[43]

2.2.1 Customer Experience

In scholarly language, customer experience refers to a business process that uses strategic management to define all customer experiences with a company, brand or product at all customer contact points. The goal of this approach is to build strong customer relationships through active experience management and thus create a significant competitive advantage for the company.[44] Customer experience has an effect on emotional consumer behaviour and is intended to provide positive experiences for customers. The successful management of these customer experiences is facilitated by the use of customer experience principles.[45] In most cases, these named experiences take place at various customer contact points. Through the use of designed experiences, customer experience should exceed the expectations of customers and companies in a cross-channel dialogue.[46] According to customer experience principles, these unexpected but positive experiences increase

---

[40] Cf. Bruhn, M., Homburg, C. (2006), p. 7
[41] Cf. Bruhn, M., Homburg, C. (2006), p. 9
[42] Cf. Leußer, W. (2011), p. 19
[43] Cf. Hippner, H. (2011), p. 249
[44] Cf. Schmitt, B., Rogers, D. (2008), pp. 698-704
[45] Cf. Peppers, D., & Rogers, M. (2016), p. 35
[46] Cf. Schmitt, Bernd. (2011), pp. 57-58

the chances of retaining customers in the long term and thus creating a more profitable customer relationship. The increased customer loyalty enables a higher level of customer satisfaction and leads to a further increase in customer profitability.[47]

While the traditional marketing approach focused on products and short-term profit maximization through planning and control, marketing culture has undergone a fundamental change with the increasing use of customer relationship management.[48] The acquisition of new customers has become increasingly less important, while long-term customer loyalty and customer satisfaction have gained in relevance greatly against the backdrop of sustainable relationship marketing.[49]

Customer experience management (CEM) can be distinguished from customer relationship management to the extent that, thanks to customer-centricity, it is an outside-in approach in which the focus is on interaction and experience orientation and qualitative data is added to the quantitative data obtained from the CRM to provide even deeper customer insight.[50] It should be noted that, despite its developing character, CEM cannot replace CRM but can only complement it in a useful way.[51]

Customer experiences can be created through direct and indirect contact points (touchpoints) with the customer. Direct touchpoints are those that can be designed and controlled by a company and include, for example, customer hotlines or websites. Indirect touchpoints, such as word-of-mouth propaganda, are difficult to influence by a company.[52] This makes it all the more important for companies to optimally design direct touchpoints along the customer journey in order to sustainably increase customer satisfaction and thus bind customers to the company in the long term.[53]

---

[47] Cf. Baran, Roger J., & Galka, Robert J. (2017), p. 86
[48] Cf. Kumar, V., & Reinartz, Werner. (2018), pp. 35-36
[49] Cf. Albach, H. (2002), pp. 22-25
[50] Cf. Herbstritt, K. (2015), pp. 11-12
[51] Cf. Herbstritt, K. (2015), pp. 13-15
[52] Cf. Meffert, H., Burmann, C., Kirchgeorg, M. (2012), pp. 208-209
[53] Cf. Yi, Youjae. (2014), p. 63

2.2.2 Customer Journey

The customer journey structures the experience flow from the customer's perspective by guiding every step a customer takes to purchase a product or consume a service.[54] The customer journey describes the continuous cycle of the relationship between a company and consumers from a customer perspective.[55] The customer journey consists of experience steps, the contact points at which the customer comes into contact with the respective experience step, and includes a view of the environment, since a customer contact point must always be integrated into the context of the entire customer journey.[56] A customer journey is the sum of customer contact points and thus represents the overall customer experience. The sum of all experiences with a brand, in turn, determines brand image and brand perception.[57] The so-called ecosystem should not be neglected, as it is only through this that the relationships and dependencies between individual experience steps become clear.[58] Connectivity across the entire customer journey requires a system-level solution.[59] In addition to the individual activities a customer experiences with the company, a customer journey view should also record what a customer sees during the experience steps and what happens behind the scenes.[60]

In the course of the ideal-typical customer journey, the selection of possible offers is systematically reduced from initial inspiration to the actual purchase. In reality, however, the decision-making process is more complex since, for example, further offers can be added in the course of the search phase and not all consumers follow a linear experience path.[61] In addition to various entry points into the customer journey, consumers also have various sources of information and channels at their disposal.[62]

A typical customer journey can be divided into the following three phases.

---

[54] Cf. Nguyen, P., Pupillo, N. (2012), pp. 318-320
[55] Cf. Buttle, Francis. (2009), pp. 34
[56] Cf. Richardson, A. (2010)
[57] Cf. Dubberly, H., Evenson, S. (2008)
[58] Cf. Manning, H., & Bodine, K. (2012), p.38
[59] Cf. Brugnoli, G. (2009)
[60] Cf. Manning, H., & Bodine, K. (2012), pp. 49-52
[61] Cf. Court, D., Elzinga, D., Mulder, S., Vetvik, O. J. (2009)
[62] Cf. Brugnoli, G. (2009)

First pre-service phase: Before actually using the service, consumers want to become informed, daydream and fantasize.[63] This first phase is valuable for the consumer in terms of stoking his anticipation.[64] One part of the first phase is awareness. In the beginning, building of awareness is about getting involved with a company's offer at all and considering it.[65] In this phase, the customer becomes aware of an offer via various media – for example through advertising or public relations, social media activities or narratives by others – and so a need arises. The next step in the first phase is research: various offers are actively compared, tried and evaluated as far as possible.[66] Here, the consumer faces the question of which is the best offer and which offer provides the best comfort and the best price. There is a danger that too much information will result in the options getting confused.[67] During the search phase it is important to provide orientation and help. In this phase, companies should convince the consumer with convincing products, attractive sales channels with simple and fast search processes and the mediation of security and trust.[68]

Second service phase: Actual interactions within the framework of use take place during the service phase.[69] The actual purchase occurs with the final decision regarding an offer.[70] Here, the consumer enters a personal or digital sales channel and asks himself the final question as to whether he needs and should buy the product. During this phase, it is essential that the (digital) salesperson can advise the consumer and dispel any doubts, present multisensual offers and make the service experience as good as possible.[71] From the company's point of view, the post-purchase phase should be aimed at creating post-purchase dissonance, i.e., subsequent doubts about the decision to eliminate.[72] Immediately after the purchase, it is important that a simple, transparent and fast process can be ensured.[73] The

---

[63] Cf. MacInnis, D. J., Price, L. L. (1987), pp. 482-483
[64] Cf. Wikström, S. (2008), p. 45
[65] Cf. Court, D., Elzinga, D., Mulder, S., Vetvik, O. J. (2009)
[66] Cf. Court, D., Elzinga, D., Mulder, S., Vetvik, O. J. (2009)
[67] Cf. Richardson, A. (2010)
[68] Cf. Hauk, J., Schulz, C. (2012), p. 391
[69] Cf. MacInnis, D. J., Price, L. L. (1987), pp. 482-483
[70] Cf. Court, D., Elzinga, D., Mulder, S., Vetvik, O. J. (2009)
[71] Cf. Esch, F.-R., Gawlowski, D., Rühl, V. (2012), p. 21
[72] Cf. Shaw, C., Ivens, J. (2002), p. 23-24
[73] Cf. Hauk, J., Schulz, C. (2012), p. 391

actual experience phase does not begin until after the customer has completed the product use or the service is consumed during the use touchpoint of phase two. Before actual use, preparation or installation steps are sometimes necessary. During use, it is important to maintain the relationship in such a way that further complementary services are offered.

Third post-service phase: After the actual service, the consumer remembers it wistfully or collects souvenirs.[74] In this phase, the customer makes an overall assessment of the service, which in turn influences expectations for future services. From a business perspective, the goal is to create a post-consumer experience that promotes loyalty so that the consumer feels connected to the brand and recommends it to others.[75] During the post-service phase, it is crucial that simple, fast and personalised support is available.[76] During each phase of the customer journey, the customer passes through various contact points, also known as customer interfaces with the brand.[77] The connection between a contact point and the customer journey can be established in such a way that an episode or phase in the customer journey is composed of a sum of contact points and all episodes result in the customer journey or transaction.[78]

2.3 Chatbots

For many people, daily or at least frequent use of the Internet is an indispensable part of their private and professional lives.[79] At many touchpoints during the customer journey, chatbots are supposed to offer the user help and to simplify handling. Even digital natives, who generally find their way around media society 2.0 well, welcome the simplification of processes through bots, because the inhibition threshold for making contact is much lower with a chatbot than with a real person.[80] Whether the bot is artificially intelligent or rule-based does not affect the user, provided that the bot meets the requirements placed on it.[81] Chatbots, which

---

[74] Cf. MacInnis, D. J., Price, L. L. (1987), pp. 482-483
[75] Cf. Dubberly, H., Evenson, S. (2008)
[76] Cf. Hauk, J., Schulz, C. (2012), p. 391
[77] Cf. Schmitt, B. H., Mangold, M. (2004), pp. 127-128
[78] Cf. Dreyer, A., Dehner, C. (2003), p. 94
[79] Cf. Sulaiman, A., Naqshbandi, M. M. (2014), p. 19
[80] Cf. Braun, A. (2003), pp. 208-209
[81] Cf. Saeed, K., Chaki, N., Pati, B., Bakshi, S., Mohapatra, D. (2018) p. 112

have already become part of our everyday lives, are often found in B2C communications, i.e., in the interactions between companies and their customers. In this case, the bots serve as digital consultants who are available at any time in the form of an avatar for queries, such as frequently asked questions (FAQs), or for better orientation on a website.[82]

The three main current applications of chatbots are extended customer service, e-commerce and information filtering.[83] In addition, they are used for pure entertainment and as text-based personal assistants. In customer service or support, bots can answer routine queries, obtain customer feedback and select escalation points at which the user is directed to a real employee.[84] By analysing a user's existing preferences and requesting information during a dialogue, the bot can give personalized purchase recommendations as part of e-commerce. In the future, it might also be possible to pay directly online via Facebook chatbots.[85] Based on information about a user, such as location and interests, it is also possible for a bot to present selected news or information.[86]

2.3.1 Definition

Chatbots, also known as 'chatterbots', 'virtual agents', 'digital assistants' and 'conversational agents', produce simulated conversations in which the human user and the chatbot communicate via text and voice messages or images.[87] A chatbot is a dialogue system that enters into a dialogue with the user within the framework of human-machine communication.[88] The term 'chatbot' consists of two parts: 'chat' stands for chatting or talking, and 'bot' is an abbreviation for robot. Chatbots are applications within the field of artificial intelligence (AI) that communicate with a chat partner in natural language and not through certain commands such as command lines.[89] The term 'chatbot' is defined in various ways in scholarship. According to Dale, the basic concept of chatbots is defined as result-oriented conversation:

---

[82] Cf. Maes, P. (2018), pp. 28-34
[83] Cf. Buxmann, P., Schmidt, H. (2019), p. 135
[84] Cf. Buxmann, P., Schmidt, H. (2019), p. 143
[85] Cf. Bager, J. (2016), p.112 - 114
[86] www.theguardian.com, 23.11.2018
[87] Cf. McTear, M., Callejas, Z., Griol, D. (2016), p. 57
[88] Cf. Eicher, D. (2016)
[89] Cf. Niegemann, H. M., Domagk, S., Hessel, S., Hein, A., Hupfer, M., Zobel, A. (2008), p. 598

their aim is to '[...] achieve some result by conversing with a machine in a dialogic fashion, using natural language'.[90] Schlicht has similarly defined a chatbot as a 'service, powered by rules and sometimes artificial intelligence, that you interact with via a chat interface'.[91] The definitions given above differ, but they all refer to the fact that chatbots are driven by AI.

For the purposes of this paper, a chatbot is defined as an intelligent software program that communicates with its user using natural language via text, voice and images. A chatbot can take complete control of an account or profile in a messaging service and react automatically to messages.

2.3.2 Conceptual Architecture

There are two differences in how chatbots are programmed. A rule-based chatbot uses an algorithm in order to provide correct answers to questions from customers by delivering an appropriate answer based on a programmed database. A self-learning chatbot learns to independently provide the right answers through conversations with people. In this case, the chatbot is artificially intelligent.[92]

Conversation with a universal chatbot, in contrast to a topic-specific chatbot, is not limited to a specific subject area.[93] For developers, this means that a chatbot must understand everything from the weather to insurance issues and solve them with confidence.[94] For humans, this gives the impression that the chatbot answers their questions spontaneously.[95] Since this work is is still developing new applications, universal chatbots are not discussed in more detail here.

Based on different user behaviour, rule-based chatbots can be divided into three types. Menu/button-based chatbots are the most basic type of chatbot on the market today.[96] In most cases, these chatbots are glorified decision-tree hierarchies presented to the user in the form of buttons. These chatbots require the user to make several selections to dig deeper towards the ultimate answer. They fall well

---

[90] Cf. Dale, R. (2016), p. 811
[91] Cf. Schlicht, M. (2016)
[92] Cf. Vogt, M. (2016)
[93] www. chatbotsmagazine.com, 23.11.2018
[94] www. medium.com, 23.11.2018
[95] Cf. Plassmann, E. (2011), p. 251
[96] www. forbes.com, 23.11.2018

short in more advanced scenarios in which there are too many variables or too much knowledge at play to reliably predict how users should reach specific answers.[97] It is also worth noting that menu/button-based chatbots are the slowest in terms of getting the user to their desired value.[98] Unlike menu-based chatbots, keyword recognition-based chatbots can observe what users type and respond appropriately – or at least try to. These chatbots utilize customizable keywords and AI to determine how to provide an appropriate response to the user.[99] For example, if a user asked the question 'What are the shipping costs to Germany?', the bot would likely use the keywords 'shipping', 'costs' and 'Germany' to best determine which answer to give. These types of chatbots fall short when they have to answer many similar questions. The chatbots will start to slip when there are keyword redundancies between several related questions. Some chatbots are a hybrid between keyword recognition-based and menu/button-based ones. These chatbots provide users with the choice to try to ask their question directly or to use the chatbot's menu buttons if the keyword recognition functionality is yielding difficult results or the user requires some guidance to find their answer. Contextual chatbots are by far the most advanced of the three types.[100] These chatbots utilize machine learning (ML) and artificial intelligence (AI) to remember conversations with specific users to learn and grow over time. Unlike keyword recognition-based chatbots, contextual chatbots are smart enough to self-improve based on what users are asking for and how they are asking it.[101] For example, a contextual chatbot that allows users to order groceries will store the data from each conversation and learn what the user likes to order. The result is that when a user chats with this chatbot, it will eventually remember their most common order, their delivery address and their payment information and merely ask if they would like to repeat this order.[102] Instead of having to respond to several questions, the user simply has to answer in the affirmative. For a contextual chatbot to be useful, a data-centric focus is imperative.[103] The goal of any chatbot should be to provide an improved

---

[97] www.chatbotslife.com, 23.11.2018
[98] www.techcrunch.com, 23.11.2018
[99] Cf. Abraham, A. (2018), p. 398
[100] Cf. Janarthanam, S. (2017), p. 192
[101] www.medium.com, 01.11.2018
[102] www.thenextweb.com, 23.11.2018
[103] Cf. Brézillon, P., Gonzalez, A. J. (2014), p. 151

user experience in comparison to the status quo. An improvement in user experience often arises from providing particular value. Leveraging conversation context is one of the best ways to shorten a process like this using a chatbot, and this could be improved by natural language processing.[104] Natural language processing (NLP), i.e., the analysis of linguistic data with the aid of calculation methods, plays an important role in interactions with chatbots.[105] By using NLP, questions on a certain topic, consisting of words, phrases and sentences, can be transferred to the computer and answered in a suitable way.[106] Chatbots are thus part of the field of artificial intelligence. Conversations are generated using a stimulus-response approach in which the user's input is compared with a large number of stored patterns from a knowledge base and a suitable response or action is produced.[107] Since the middle of the 20th century, AI has been regarded as a field of science in its own right.[108] In order to imitate human intelligence, researchers are striving to use algorithms to develop programs that can deliver this kind of performance. The most elementary requirements for a chatbot are responsiveness – a chatbot must respond to input from the user – and autonomy, as a chatbot must be able to process or answer inputs independently.[109]

Using AI, chatbots can forecast, understand and execute multi-level and complex user requests.[110] So far, most conversations with chatbots have been text-based, although some newer chatbots use voice and image recognition as input and output.[111]

2.3.3 Conversational Interfaces

A conversational interface is a user interface with which a user interacts when communicating with a device or a system.[112] Conversational interfaces are often coupled with chatbots or intelligent personal assistants (IPAs). An IPA is a software

---

[104] Cf. Hoffmann, A. (2018), pp. 111-118
[105] Cf. Verspoor K., Cohen K.B. (2013), p. 1494
[106] Cf. Goksel Canbek, N., Mutlu, M. E. (2016), p. 595
[107] Cf. McTear, M., Callejas, Z., Griol, D. (2016), pp. 125-148
[108] Cf. Ertel, W. (2016), p. 6
[109] Cf. www.deloitte.com, 23.11.2018
[110] Cf. Goksel Canbek, N., Mutlu, M. E. (2016), p. 595
[111] Cf. McTear, M., Callejas, Z., Griol, D. (2016), p. 57
[112] Cf. McTear, M., Callejas, Z., Griol, D. (2016), pp. 125-148

agent that can perform tasks or services for a person. These tasks or services are based on user input, location conditions and the ability to access information from a variety of online sources. The user often interacts with an IPA via a conversational interface, and companies such as Google with its assistant, Apple with Siri, Microsoft with Cortana and Amazon with Alexa have developed their own IPAs based on conversational interfaces. Since IPAs can perform other tasks on devices, it should be noted that a chatbot is the part of an IPA that represents the entire conventional interaction. The chatbot generates natural reactions to human user text input.[113] Chatbots are designed to make users believe that they are talking to someone else.[114] To date, most chatbots are text-based, but speech input has evolved as a new recognition technology. More and more chatbots use speech as input and output.[115] A chatbot reacts to input commands without being the initiator of a conversation. According to McTear, the conversational interface of a chatbot should work as follows: The chatbot recognizes the text sent by the user. The chatbot understands the words and interprets them to determine the context. An answer is formulated or, if the original message was unclear, further interaction with the user takes place until the context is clarified. A response is presented in the form of words or other file formats, such as images.[116]

Chatbots differ primarily in terms the platform for which they are designed. Platforms are online ecosystems where chatbots can be used to interact with users and perform actions for users.[117] Some of the most popular platforms include Facebook Messenger, WhatsApp, WeChat, Skype, SMS, Slack, Google Allo and Kik, but an individual website can also be used as a platform for chatbots.[118] When considering chatbot ecosystems, it is important to distinguish between platforms and development frameworks.[119] Development frameworks, such as Microsoft Bot Framework, Amazon Lex, Facebook's Wit, Dexter, Google's Dialogflow, are used to build and define the behaviour of chatbots.[120] Platforms and frameworks are directly related,

---

[113] Cf. Smolinski, R., Gerdes, M., Siejka, M., Bodek, M. (2017), p. 211
[114] www.medium.com, 13.11.2018
[115] www.theguardian.com, 23.11.2018
[116] Cf. McTear, M., Callejas, Z., Griol, D. (2016), pp. 125-148
[117] www.chatbotslife.com, 23.11.2018
[118] www.chatbotsjournal.com, 23.11.2018
[119] Cf. Janarthanam, S. (2017), p. 204
[120] www.geekflare.com, 23.11.2018

but distinguishing the two is important. In addition to frameworks, NLP engines, such as Google Platform Speech, and natural language APIs, such as IBM Watson or Microsoft LUIS, can be used.[121] The main task of an NLP engine is to understand user input and translate it into computer language.[122] The bot is taught to extract useful information from written or spoken language and convert it into structured data. Most of the biggest bot platform players engage in different areas – for example, Microsoft uses Cortana as a virtual assistant, offers a platform to deploy bots on Skype, provides NLP as a service with LUIS and also offers a framework for building bots. The advanced technologies of development frameworks and NLP engines involve coding or configuring technical tools, but they are often more powerful than providers. Chatbot providers offer code-free technologies which enable anyone to modify the bot with a graphic interface using drag-and-drop but which can be less customizable. Popular providers include Chatfuel, flow.ai, Converse.ai, reply.aiM and FlowXO.[123] In addition, providers often specialize in certain industries or core topics, such as e-commerce or customers.

Since this thesis does not discuss the technical background of chatbots but rather their commercial use, the following chapters deal with chatbot providers and highlight the extensive benefits of chatbots.

---

[121] www.chatbotsmagazine.com, 01.11.2018
[122] Cf. Rashid, K., Das, A. (2017), p. 84
[123] www.analyticsinsight.net, 23.11.2018

3 Chatbots in E-Commerce

3.1 Implementation throughout the Customer Journey

To conduct a systematic investigation of individual purchasing decision behaviour, decision processes can be observed over time. Phase models allow for consumers' purchasing decisions to be viewed as a process with various stages, which are gradually progressed through. A widespread standard model consists of five steps: problem identification, information search, evaluation of alternatives, purchase decision and subsequent purchase behaviour.[124]

For cognitively controlled purchases in online environments, Patwardhan and Ramaprasad have proposed a reduced but, in principle, comparable process model.[125] The model comprises the phases of pre-emption search/evaluation, purchase/use and post-acquisition interaction. Hoffmann and Nowak agree with the aforementioned authors that habitual models of decision-making behaviour can also be applied to consumers' purchasing decision behaviour on the Internet.[126] Peterson, Balasurbramanian and Bronenberg have emphasized in particular the influence of the Internet on purchasing decision behaviour.[127] With expanded access to information, consumers can better adapt their information acquisition to different starting points. This basic structure, which is explicitly extended by the Internet in the information phase and by personality traits in the evaluation phase, can also be found in the work of Smith and Rupp.[128]

3.1.1 Information and Product Research

There is a discrepancy between the actual condition and the desired condition of a consumer, which is noticed by the consumer. This can be due to internal or external stimuli.[129] An internal stimulus can be, for example, the feeling of hunger, which is solved by food intake. External stimuli can be influenced by marketing. An important goal of marketing is to identify external stimuli, e.g., communication

---

[124] Cf. Kotler, Keller und Bliemel 2007, p. 296-306
[125] Cf. Patwardhan, P., Ramaprasad, J. (2005), p. 5
[126] Cf. Hoffman, D., Novak, T. (1998), p. 10
[127] Cf. Peterson, R., Balasubramanian, S., Bronnenberg, B. (1997), p. 339
[128] Cf. Smith, A., Rupp, W. (2003), p. 424
[129] Cf. Tyagi, C.L., Kumar A. (2001), pp. 55-57

measures that arouse the consumer's interest in a particular product category or product.[130]

Depending on the importance of the decision, consumers become more or less active in order to obtain additional information regarding the intended purchase decision. Sources of information can be personal (family, colleagues, neighbour, friends), commercial (e.g., webshops, advertising), public (e.g., mass media and testing institutes) or based on experience (e.g., touching the product and trying it out).[131]

In the information and product research phase, it is important for the potential customer to obtain information about the supplier and the product which is suitable to satisfy his specific needs.[132] System support can be provided by directory services and electronic product catalogues. The Internet offers numerous possibilities to use product information, such as product properties, images, information about material composition and manufacturing process, instructions for use and customer evaluations and recommendations.[133] For an online retailer, this information must be made available either in the online shop or at other touchpoints. In addition to the actual products and their availability, ancillary information such as payment and delivery terms are of great importance for a potential buyer.[134] The confidence on a safe completion should also be mediated in this phase already. The online shop is a central medium here; however, other touchpoints, such as social media or a newsletter, can also support communications. Changing touchpoints is very easy and fast, and buyers in e-commerce often visit several channels of the retailer before making their purchase.[135] Chatbots can be used at any touchpoint. They can react individually to any inquiries or actively provide suggestions for products and information about them.[136] Lego, for example, uses a Facebook Messenger chatbot that provides a great deal of information even before you visit the online shop: Parents and relatives receive tips on the right Christmas present. The chatbot, named 'Ralph', asks the user various questions. In addition to the age of

---

[130] Cf. Blythe, J. (2012), p. 56
[131] Cf. Kotler, P. (2013), p. 179
[132] Cf. Ingram, T. N., LaForge, R. W., Avila, R. A., Schwepker, C. H., Williams, M. R. (2015), p. 60
[133] Cf. Heinemann, G. (2018), p. 53
[134] Cf. Gast, O. (2018), pp. 13-15
[135] Cf. Kruse Brandão, T., Wolfram, G. (2018), pp. 10-11
[136] Cf. Möbus, et al. (2006), p. 51

the person receiving the present, he also wants to know more about the recipient. To acquire this information, he suggests different categories of characterization, for example 'always creating something new'. He also asks about the available budget. At the end, the bot introduces several sets of Lego, which the user can buy immediately. The user is forwarded to the online shop for this purpose.

Figure 1: Lego's Facebook Messenger Chatbot

Argomall, a supplier of electronic objects from the Philippines, explains the terms of delivery and payment on Facebook Messenger in addition to product information:

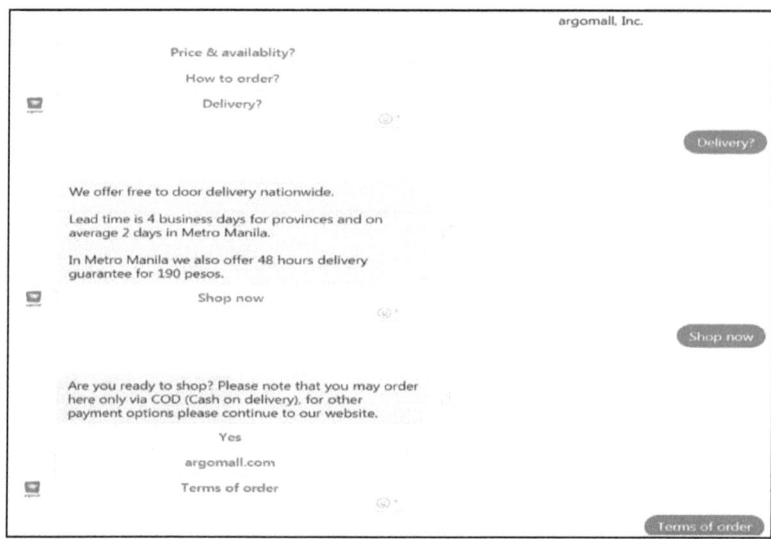

Figure 2: Argomall's Facebook Messenger Chatbot

Chatbots on social media platforms such as Facebook can thus communicate directly with users through ads from the first point of contact, and they can share all the necessary information needed regarding a potential purchase without the user having to change channels.[137]

3.1.2 Consideration and Purchase

It is often assumed that consumers perceive a product as a bundle of properties. Individual product attributes are assigned different utility values, and each product with unique attribute characteristics satisfies consumer needs to varying degrees.[138] The evaluation of alternatives can therefore be characterized by ambivalence and uncertainty.[139]

In the consideration phase, an attitude towards product alternatives has been formed as a result of evaluating the alternatives, and a purchase intention has been formulated, but external factors can still influence the purchase decision.[140] For

---

[137] Cf. Hoffmann, A. (2018), p. 61
[138] Cf. Broeckelmann, P. (2010), p. 162
[139] Cf. Peter, J. P., Olson, J. C. (1999), pp. 166-168
[140] Cf. Runia, P., Wahl, F., Geyer, O., Thewißen, C. (2015), pp. 23-26

example, third parties such as opinion leaders can sway the decision in one direction or the other.[141] Unforeseen situational factors can also change the purchase decision, for example when a washing machine breaks down unexpectedly and the planned purchase of a new television set is postponed.[142] Purchase decisions are also subject to a evaluation of purchase risk, depending on the significance of the purchase.

In the purchase phase, a distinction can be made between the agreement phase and the settlement phase.[143] In the agreement phase, an attempt is made to reach agreement on the terms and conditions under which a legally valid purchase agreement can be concluded.[144] While often only a price and condition policy based on a 'take it or leave it' principle is supported, some systems allow customer-specific discount rates, payment procedures and payment periods, etc., to be applied on the basis of stored profile information.

In the settlement phase, the last phase of the business transaction, the actual processing of the purchase contract takes place.[145] In the case of physical goods, it is also necessary to agree on a transit procedure and any transport insurance in addition to a method of payment. A service should also be provided that allows the current delivery status to be tracked.

There are two ways to map these phases for an online shop. During so-called checkout, which represents a virtual checkout in e-commerce, the customer is asked to choose his preferred payment method and enter his address.[146] One option is the one-page checkout. This conveniently displays all the steps of the order process on one page. The customer does not have to wait for the page to reload; he automatically jumps from step to step during the one-page checkout.[147] The obvious disadvantage of one-page checkouts lies in their limited space: if merchants ask for much information on a single page at one time, this can visually overwhelm the customer to such an extent that he no longer feels like shopping. The density of information

---

[141] Cf. Peter, J. P., Olson, J. C. (1999), pp. 166-168
[142] Cf. Rutschmann, M. (2018), p. 82
[143] Cf. Schubert, P., Selz, D. (2007), p. 85
[144] Cf. Hougaard, S., & Bjerre, M. (2002), p. 97
[145] Cf. Schubert, P., Selz, D. (2007), p. 85
[146] Cf. Heinemann, G. (2018), pp. 94-95
[147] Cf. Solomon, M. R. (2015), p. 357

can also lead to confusion and thus to errors and frustrations during the filling-in process. Multi-stage checkouts divide the individual steps – personal data, shipping addresses and information, payment information and order overview – into individual steps and thus into individual pages.[148] This makes the individual pages clearer and easier to use. Multi-stage checkouts, however, are more complicated to operate on a mobile phone than on a PC screen. In addition, typical performance problems are avoided by accidentally clicking back and forth between the form pages.

A chatbot can combine both aspects described above. The user can remain within the conversational interface of the chatbot, as during a one-page checkout, but the information can be queried step by step, as during a multi-stage checkout.[149] Online shops such as 1-800-Flowers.com, an online shop for bouquets, show the way:

---

[148] Cf. Kollewe, T., Keukert, M. (2016), p. 225
[149] www.chatbotsmagazine.com, 27.11.2018

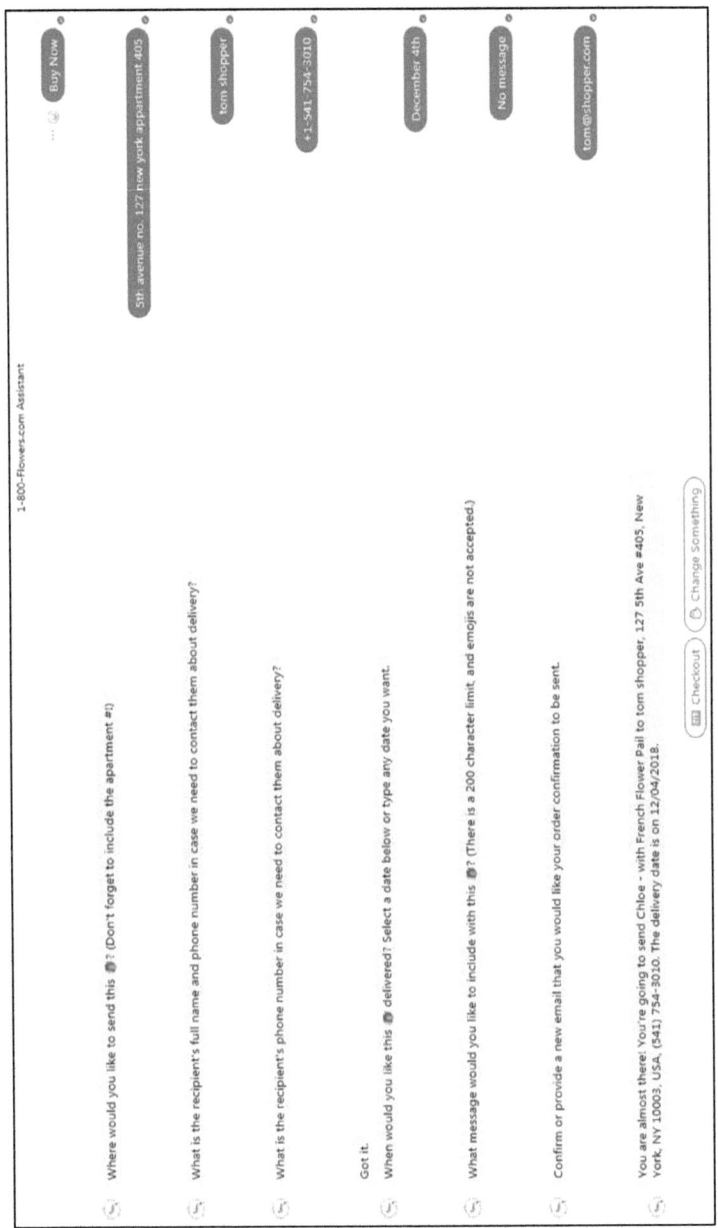

Figure 3: 1-800-Flowers.com Facebook Messenger Chatbot

The 1-800-Flowers.com store on Facebook Messenger makes it possible to order a bouquet directly using the chat. Chatbots enable customers to make purchases on social media platforms without having to change channels.[150]

3.1.3 Retention and Loyalty in After-sale Phase

Usually, buyers decide whether they are dissatisfied, satisfied or even enthusiastic only after the purchase and use of a product. Truthful communication about product performance avoids excessive expectations that could lead to disappointment. Manufacturers or sellers can reduce the problem of post-purchase dissonance through guarantees and letters of confirmation.[151]

During the after-sale phase, customers continue to be supported even after the purchase of a product in order to strengthen customer loyalty.[152] This starts with customers being given the opportunity to check the delivery status of their order online. Along with the delivery of the goods, additional services are available to the customer. Many of these services, e.g., complaint management, instructions for use and user tips, can be carried out electronically. If, however, the customer's problem cannot be solved using general information, the use of service personnel, e.g., in the form of a service hotline, is indispensable. A particular challenge during this process phase is managing the return of goods.[153] In addition to the planning and organization of return transport, reverse processing of the payment must also be guaranteed.[154]

During this phase, chatbots can provide a variety of information from various systems in order to provide customers with a transparent process.[155] The bot can respond to the individual needs and requests of users in real time.[156] In addition, chatbots can learn from a customer's purchase history and make recommendations at the right time for subsequent purchases to ensure retention.[157] In contrast to a customer service centre, chatbots are not tied to specific working hours and

---

[150] www.chatbotslife.com, 27.11.2018
[151] Cf. McDaniel, C. D., Lamb, C. W., Hair, J. F. (2012), p. 146
[152] Cf. Cf. Peter, J. P., Olson, J. C. (1999), pp. 211-217
[153] Cf. Heinemann, G. (2018), pp. 108-109
[154] Cf. Kollewe, T., Keukert, M. (2016), p. 271
[155] Cf. www.ecommerce-chatbots.com, 27.11.2018
[156] Cf. www.deloitte.com, 23.11.2018
[157] www.chatbotslife.com, 29.11.2018

serve the customer throughout the day and react more quickly to inquiries.[158] Conversation can take place using chatbots that are either integrated into platforms, such as WhatsApp or Facebook Messenger, or which can be found as stand-alone services on a company's website. The chat conversations can include product advice, support for the sales process and purchases, and customer support to facilitate consumption by the customer.[159] Since the customer interacts with the company or brand in the same way as with a friend, the term 'brand as a friend' is also used.[160] This is why companies whose chatbots can have conversations that feel natural and human-like to the user benefit.[161] In addition to FAQs and product advice, the chatbot named Clara on the website Otto.de can provide information about the status of an order. In addition to tracking a shipment, a return can be requested or a setup service can be arranged:

---

[158] www.inc.com, 19.12.2018
[159] Cf. Braun, A. (2003), p. 28
[160] www.ey.com, 29.11.2018
[161] www.wired.com, 29.11.2018

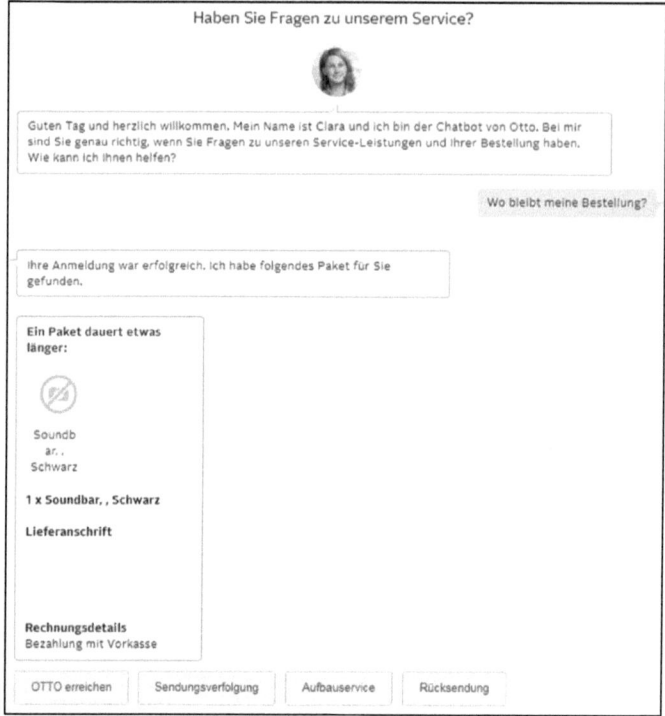

Figure 4: Otto.de Onlineshop Chatbot "Clara"

In addition to the fast response time of chatbots, there are other benefits that are discussed on an ongoing basis.

3.2 Opportunities

A big advantage of using chatbots is that companies can use their services where the majority of users spend time such as in the messaging and social network apps. Facebook Messenger had 1.3 billion globally active users per month in September 2017.[162] In theory, companies can reach this total number with a chatbot that is integrated into the messenger service. This potential is further supported by Deloitte's prediction that 95 per cent of the 100 best software companies will have

---

[162] www.statista.com, 29.11.2018

integrated one or more cognitive technologies, such as IBM Watson, by 2020.[163] According to Harkous, a researcher at the Laboratory of Distributed Information Systems (LSIR) some market analysts believe that chatbots will become a multi-vendor tool for the information technology industry and a billion dollar market.[164]

3.2.1 Customer Experience

Every product and every service is an experience for connected customers. This also applies to interactions with a company. The customer experience plays a central role on the market which is always supported by competition between exchangeable products and services.[165] A company can differentiate itself and win long-term customer loyalty on the basis of a positive customer experience at various contact points. Especially against the background of dwindling loyalty rates and an increasing willingness to change, the customer experience is becoming increasingly important.[166] An Omnichannel offering, which offers a wide range of contact options, leads to an extension of the customer experience.[167] Chatbots can not only help to save costs but also to eliminate insecurities and obstacles for customers. Due to ignorance on the part of some customers on the World Wide Web and their excessive demands on the navigation of Internet pages, shopping processes are sometimes interrupted. According to Buschmann, dialogue systems can make a valuable contribution to minimizing the problem of such abandoned shopping carts.[168] According to the Futurecom E-Commerce Study, 25 per cent of Swiss customers hesitate to use an online shop because they do not trust it. Nearly 40 per cent of those surveyed said that they had cancelled their online-shopping visit because they could not find what they were looking for due to the confusing presentation of a website.[169] In such cases, customers do not enjoy the act of making a purchase, and this is a factor that companies cannot ignore because the emotional experience, the customer experience, plays a key role in purchasing decisions.[170]

---

[163] www.deloitte.com, 30.11.2018
[164] Cf. Crivelli, G. (2016)
[165] Cf. Meffert, H., Bruhn, M., Hadwich, & Karsten. (2015), p. 200
[166] Cf. Holland, H., Ramanathan, N. (2016), pp. 187-189
[167] www.computerworld.com, 30.11.2018
[168] Cf. Buschmann, M. (2003), p. 105
[169] www.futurecom.ch, 30.11.2018
[170] Cf. Stricker, A. (2003), p. 172

For a young target group, Facebook Messenger, WhatsApp, etc., are already the primary contact channels. This contributes, among other things, to the fact that the future of customer service and advice will look more digital and automated.[171] At the same time, people's communication behaviour has changed. Questions are entered into Google and the search engine provides an answer. The rest, e.g., navigating through a website, filling out a contact form or conducting other search actions, must be done by the user independently. Customers who are overburdened with digital technology and cannot find their way around websites face a great challenge to going online at all.[172]

In view of the flood of information people are confronted with today, chatbots can to a certain extent take responsibility and contribute to reducing complexity, taking away the customer's feeling of loneliness and reducing barriers. The customer receives a personal response and the chatbot helps to solve the problem. In addition to responding directly to customer requests, chatbots can pull up the pages customers are looking for in parallel and guide customers directly to the desired information.[173] Once the customer has made use of the services of a chatbot, he or she will most likely contact him or her again in the event of a later problem or visit to the website, provided that the interaction has been positive. In the best case, the customer likes the chatbot, which can lead to a recommendation to friends, acquaintances and/or family.[174]

The active use of chatbots is still not widespread, with only on average one in six having already used a chatbot. According to Bitkom Research, however, 41 per cent of the 1,000 respondents who want to use chatbots can very well imagine using chatbots for customer service.[175] This number will probably dramatically grow in the future.[176] If a chatbot has already been implemented on a messenger platform, such as Facebook or Microsoft, it is easier for users to chat with the chatbot on the messenger app already installed on their smartphone instead of having to download a new app again and again.[177] In a survey conducted by Fittkau & Maass

---

[171] www.statista.com, 30.11.2018
[172] www.magronet.de, 30.11.2018
[173] Cf. Braun, A. (2003), p. 35
[174] Cf. Stricker, A. (2003), pp. 172-175
[175] www.statista.com, 01.12.2018
[176] www.statista.com, 30.11.2018
[177] Cf. Crivelli, G. (2016)

Consulting, just under 40 per cent of respondents said they could imagine using chatbots because they would receive a quick answer to their question.[178] This makes it clear that chatbots provide respite for customer service staff and that customers do not have to wait too long in a queue. The following figure shows what chatbots can be used for from the customer's point of view:

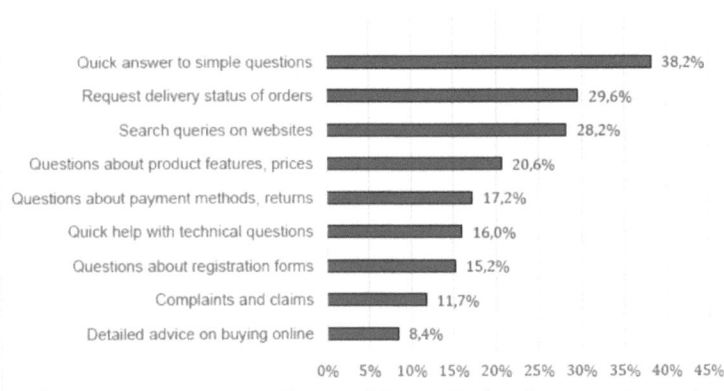

Figure 5: Trends in usage behavior – Fittkau & Maass Consulting[179]

Furthermore, an additional study which was also published in 2016, showed that the average satisfaction rate of consumers with chatbots and intelligent assistants was 65 per cent. Among those who did not believe they had ever interacted with a chatbot, the expected satisfaction with chat friendliness was 45 per cent. Friendliness, ease of use and speed were rated as the best.[180]

3.2.2 Gaining Customer Knowledge

When visiting the website, customers leave behind a variety of data that the company can use to obtain relevant information about user behaviour, or to obtain information about their needs. The use of chatbots provides an optimal and simple basis for effective market research.[181] The conversations conducted are

---

[178] www.fittkaumaass.de, 01.12.2018
[179] www.fittkaumaass.de, 01.12.2018
[180] www.aspect.com, 01.12.2018
[181] Cf. Braun, A. (2003), p. 38

automatically documented and recorded, and they provide a source of information about the customer's thinking.[182] This is of great importance for customer relationship management. By evaluating log files, requirements can be recorded and thus processed more efficiently.[183]

In addition, chatbots enable the storage of cookies, and the user can be recognized as soon as the website is visited again. A website can thus be optimized to the individual needs of the customers. While the completion of online surveys is usually too monotonous, a chatbot can be used to stimulate the process. Through the simulation of a human conversation partner, a higher involvement can be generated than would be possible in a static environment.[184] Another advantage is the possibility to check the quality of the dialogue. If the level of conversation between the chatbot and the customer drops or the knowledge of the chatbot reaches its limit, the enterprise can do this during an analysis of the dialogue. This allows any gaps in knowledge to be identified and customer conversations to be improved.[185]

3.2.3 Cross Selling

In addition to passively answering specific customer concerns, proactive chatbots can intervene in the sales process with the aim of creating additional sales incentives.[186] The chatbot creates direct access to company services and products and thereby opens up cross-selling opportunities for companies.[187] The cross-selling strategy uses empirical values collected via an affinity cluster. This makes it relatively easy to determine whether customers who are interested in a particular product and have even already bought it are also accessible to incentives to buy from other product groups. This collection of empirical values enables a knowledge database to be built.[188]

As already mentioned, a virtual advisor can use cookies stored by the chatbot to access the customer's activities and information. The chatbot recognizes the

---

[182] Cf. Meffert, H., Bruhn, M., Hadwich, & Karsten. (2015), pp. 208-209
[183] Cf. Bange, C., Schinzer, H. (2005), p. 54
[184] Cf. Braun, A. (2003), p. 39
[185] Cf. Samuelsen, P. (2003), p. 32
[186] www.jekelteam.de, 01.12.2018
[187] www.ibm.com, 01.12.2018
[188] Cf. Buschmann, M. (2003), p. 105

customer's intention and gives him or her the possibility to buy suitable products from the company's product range.[189]

3.2.4 Cost Efficiency

The use of chatbots offers companies an opportunity to cut costs. Customers expect a service that is available around the clock and on all channels.[190] This constant need for availability and help anytime and anywhere would overburden customer service and, above all, would be simply too expensive.[191] Companies that have implemented a chat solution in customer service are recording a reduction in incoming calls and e-mails of up to 10 to 30 per cent.[192] In his model calculation, Buschmann calculated the processing costs of an entire customer inquiry via e-mail as 10 euros.[193] This figure, however, is strongly dependent on the employee's level of qualification and can therefore vary. Assuming these estimated processing costs of 10 euros, 100 e-mail inquiries per day would result in an annual cost of 365,000 euros. With the introduction of a dialogue system, a 20 per cent reduction in income would result in proportional savings of 73,000 euros.[194] Chatbots can reduce the number of requests for which the answers are similar or even identical within a very short time. Depending on the industry, 50–70 per cent of customer requests are standard questions that can be answered based on a stored database or by a chatbot without any loss of quality.[195] In addition, customer service employees are given sufficient time to address more complex issues. As a result, value-adding activities can be increased and generate added value for the company.[196] It has to be noted that the use of chatbots leads to decreasing call volumes and thus better accessibility, and it relieves the burden on the call centre. This aspect correlates with an increase in customer satisfaction, since customers can be served faster and more efficiently. The relocation of human support into a virtual environment shows how, as already explained above, the potential of cost reduction and

---

[189] Cf. Stricker, A. (2003), pp. 180-185
[190] Cf. Franke, M., & Schulz, C. (2016), p. 93
[191] www.forbes.com, 01.12.2018
[192] Cf. Langer, C. (2016), p. 40
[193] Cf. Meffert, H., Bruhn, M., Hadwich, & Karsten. (2015), pp. 208-209
[194] Cf. Buschmann, M. (2003), p. 103
[195] Cf. Buschmann, M. (2003), p. 102
[196] www.accenture.com, 01.12.2018

efficiency increase due to today's transparent markets, customer orientation has become a key success factor.[197] The marketing strategies of companies have changed from maximizing profit from individual sales to long-term business relationships and striving for customer loyalty.[198] Today, a diverse range of customer services is of central importance for many companies. Customer care is a necessary prerequisite for creating customer loyalty, which in turn reduces acquisition costs.[199] Long-term customer loyalty is also necessary because it is far costlier to acquire new customers than to retain existing ones.[200] For this reason, it is understandable that initial investments in the development of customer relationships as well as the running costs and maintenance of chatbots can be expected to increase over time. The more satisfied a customer is with a product or service, the more frequently he or she will use that product or service and, in the best-case scenario, recommend it to others. As a result, companies will generate more follow-up purchases.[201] The uncomplicated way in which a chatbot conducts conversations with customers can have a positive effect on a company's image. In contrast to human employees, a chatbot is never in a bad mood and is always available to customers in a friendly manner.[202] One essential point should not be neglected, however: namely being able to correctly estimate the effort involved in maintaining chatbots. Knowledge databases must be created in advance and updated regularly. In order for chatbots to function properly, IT staff must constantly program new dialogues that can answer customer queries in a friendly manner.[203] All these tasks cost the company time and money.

---

[197] Cf. Meffert, H., Bruhn, M., Hadwich, & Karsten. (2015), pp. 208-209
[198] Cf. Hildebrand, V. G. (2000), p. 56
[199] Cf. Buschmann, M. (2003), p. 102
[200] Cf. Stojek, M. (2000), p. 42
[201] Cf. Gouthier, M. (2016), p. 33
[202] www.ccw.eu, 01.12.2018
[203] www.ccw.eu, 02.12.2018

4 Practical Use Case Analysis and Implementation

4.1 Collection and Selection of Use Cases

In order to generate ideas for the use of chatbots, one can use a variety of common creativity methods. This thesis will not take a closer look at brainstorming and design thinking, as every project and every company should use its own proven methods. This has no relevant effect on chatbot's idea generation.

Chatbots can be used for customer service or product search. For customer service, it is important that the bot is very intelligent and already knows a large amount of data so that every customer, also a very unclear or angry one, is understood, because a misunderstanding could lead to severe errors or customer loss. This problem, however, is solved by today's AI and machine learning possibilities.[204]

As the main research question is how to implement a possible (low-risk) use case in the context of e-commerce, it is necessary to concentrate on one use case and to analyze it regarding the conditions, the requirements for the bot, etc. Trying to create multiple bots would be too complex, time-consuming and, most importantly, not reasonable.

In order to improve the customer experience for existing customers, it makes sense to answer their questions in a familiar digital environment. With 1.5 billion daily users worldwide Facebook is the most widespread social medium and available on many mobile devices.[205] An e-commerce company can reach a large number of its customers on Facebook. The primary goal for a company should initially be comprehensive FAQs and customer service for existing orders. To achieve this goal, requirements for a social chatbot, which can respond to questions about order status and products, process returns, and enter general order conditions on the basis of a query of the customer data, are developed in the following sections.

4.2 Requirements

As productivity is the most frequent reason to use chatbots, a bot should be as productive as possible. It should provide an advantage over regular customer service. Ideally, it should be fast and also as accurate as possible. If every second question

---

[204] www.statsbot.co, 03.12.2018
[205] www.statista.com, 03.12.2018

is answered incorrectly by the bot, the customer will likely not use it again in the future. Of course, this productivity is limited to topics related to the data management of an e-commerce company.

In addition to general requirements, the design of the bot is decisive. It is important that the bot can give human-like answers and have a human-like conversation.[206] This also includes the requirement that the conversation not be one-sided and that the bot also ask questions, for example 'Can I help you?', 'Do you want to know something else?' or 'Do you understand me?' To create an environment as real and pleasant as possible for the user, the bot should also have a name and address the user with his or her name.[207]

Some requirements are summarized below.

Productivity:

- advantage over general search systems
- correct answers
- short response times

Human-like conversation:

- personal characteristics
- positive politeness
- responds to individual and personal inquiries

There are also some risks:

- The bot does not understand the user's input and therefore has to inquire multiple times. In the end, the bot gives an incorrect answer to, for example, where to find products in the online shop.
- The bot answers after a few seconds when the user is already impatient.
- The first two risks combined will probably keep the user from using the bot because it does not offer any benefit but costs a large amount of time.

---

[206] www.theguardian.com, 23.11.2018
[207] www.chatbotslife.com, 03.12.2018

- The bot answers in a manner that is too robot-like, so that the user does not have the experience of a real and good conversation. For example, the bot might simply provide the link to an online shop without further explanation.
- The bot does not have any personal information about the customer.

As there are many different ways to communicate and to ask questions, it is not possible to know all sentences at first. Nevertheless, it is helpful to think about some questions and possible bot answers before starting to implement the bot. To do this, one important 'welcome message', which is sent to every new visitor by the chatbot, has to be analyzed. The following is a small selection of the questions:

- Where is my order?
- How do I return an item?
- When will my return be refunded?
- How do I receive new return documents?
- Where can I find shoes?
- What is the outstanding amount I have to pay?
- Until when can I return my order?
- How does the shipping work?
- Can I deliver to a Packstation?
- What are the shipping costs?
- I want to cancel my order.
- How do I change my address?
- Where can I find my customer number and what do I need it for?
- What is the offer of the day?
- When will the item be available again?
- How can I reach customer service by phone?
- Do you have a branch or a shop where I can shop?
- I don't want to receive a newsletter anymore, what do I have to do?

The requirements for the bot, the risks which need to be avoided and many questions and possible bot answers are clear now. The next step is to get familiar with bot services, try to implement a bot and then compare and evaluate the services.

4.2.1 System Selection

Big companies such as Microsoft, Google, Amazon and Facebook offer bot services where people can develop chatbots adjusted to their own individual needs and applications.[208] Smaller companies or start-ups in the field of AI also offer websites, such as Chatfuel, flow.ai, Converse.ai, reply.aiM and FlowXO, where one can develop a bot without knowledge about coding.[209]

The approach of this thesis and the requirements mean that two services should be tested: Chatfuel and FlowXO are the ones selected.

Chatfuel

With simple editing elements, multi-user accounts, neuro-linguistic programming (NLP) and seamless third-party integration and analysis technology, Chatfuel aims to provide users with a simple yet effective messenger development solution. Chatfuel's editing tools allow users without programming skills to easily design chatbots. The Chatfuel dashboard allows users to determine the conversation rules used by their chatbot. These pre-defined rules allow each chatbot to productively understand and respond to user requests by using recognition. Synchronization with Facebook, Twitter and Dropbox takes place automatically. Chatfuel offers a free trial and costs $15 per month for unlimited users and messages.[210]

FlowXO FlowXO's service is similar to Chatfuel: they also say that users can easily create text-based bots that humans can chat with on their preferred interfaces – Facebook Messenger, Slack, Twilio SMS, Telegram or an existing website. Testing FlowXO is also free, and the standard plan with 5,000 interactions costs $19 per month.[211]

---

[208] www.geekflare.com, 23.11.2018
[209] www.analyticsinsight.net, 23.11.2018
[210] www.chatfuel.com, 23.11.2018
[211] www.flowxo.com, 23.11.2018

Benefit Analysis

A benefit analysis should be used to make a comparison between the two services. Evaluation criteria for an analysis are:

- Usability: Is the service user-friendly and easy to use? Can beginners start development intuitively? Is detailed documentation included and easy to understand?
- Testing of the bot: Is it possible to test the created bots directly? Can all scenarios be tested during this phase?
- Velocity: Is the service fast and reliable? Are there any errors?
- Efficiency: How much effort is necessary to obtain a good result?
- Pricing: Are the costs justified? Is the underlying value added by the services higher than the costs?

To evaluate the usability of the services, it is necessary to create an account or log in with an existing Facebook or Google account. FlowXO provides a tour, which can be skipped. The tour explains all the elements and modules on the website. Chatfuel does not offer a tour at the start. Documentation is very important for successfully developing a bot, especially for someone who has never used the service before. The documentation offered by Chatfuel is good; there are also examples of how to create the different intents, entities, etc. FlowXO also provides good documentation with step-by-step instructions which make it easy to get started. In addition, a community answers individual questions. Chatfuel offers premade templates to get started. The multitude of elements for editing these is difficult to manage without documentation. FlowXO, on the other hand, guides the user through the creation of the first template, so that one can start editing immediately.

Both tools offer test interfaces that make it possible to test the bot directly on the selected platform, such as Facebook. No configuration on Facebook is necessary; the user only has to log in. Several scenarios can be tested.

No abnormalities regarding response times and speeds were noticeable in the tests done on both platforms, nor were there any errors. Both services can be tested free of charge and have automated interfaces with platforms. Due to the large number of integrations of external services to Google products, FlowXO makes it easier to integrate a large amount of data. The multitude of configuration options offered by Chatfuel makes setting up a bot quickly more difficult. Both services allow the user to develop a mature chatbot with relatively little effort. Both services offer a free trial. The costs depend strongly on the selected use cases. Chatfuel is cheaper for the use of a reach-strong chatbot. FlowXO is slightly easier to handle and offers more integrations, and so this service is used for the following implementation.

4.3 Implementation

After registration, an introduction tour takes place. First, the column entitled 'flow' is explained. Using this function, chatbots can be created and the conversation with the users defined. The column 'bots' enables integration into individual platforms; a bot can be integrated into different platforms. Using 'broadcasts', messages can be sent to the users of the chatbot, independently of the chatbot. The integrated live chat allows humans to intervene in chatbot conversations and actively advertise customer service. Information about users can be viewed under 'users'. With the 'interactions' function, conversations can be filtered and searched. 'Analytics' can be used to analyze general metrics, and 'webtools' can be used to advertise the created chatbots elsewhere.

Clicking 'flow' '+ new bot' and selecting a platform creates a new chatbot. After entering the chatbot name, its integration into Facebook can take place. By clicking on 'login to Facebook' and using the following Facebook menu, the creator can select an existing Facebook page or create a new one. On the following page, 'test & distribute' or 'message us' can be selected. After confirmation, the platform is connected to the flow. In order to interact with users, the flow must now be established. Every flow starts with a trigger. A trigger tells the chatbot what user input to listen for. The flow will begin when the user's input matches the trigger.

For example, a user could type, 'How do I receive a new return label?' If this matches the trigger, the bot will start the flow. Alternatively, the user could be given to option to press a button that will trigger the flow. Clicking '+' creates the trigger. The bot can be selected in the 'choose a service' window, and 'new message' can be selected as the trigger. The new message window displays options for the trigger to define when to start the flow. The text that a user can type to trigger a flow needs to be defined. It is possible to add one word or phrase per line:

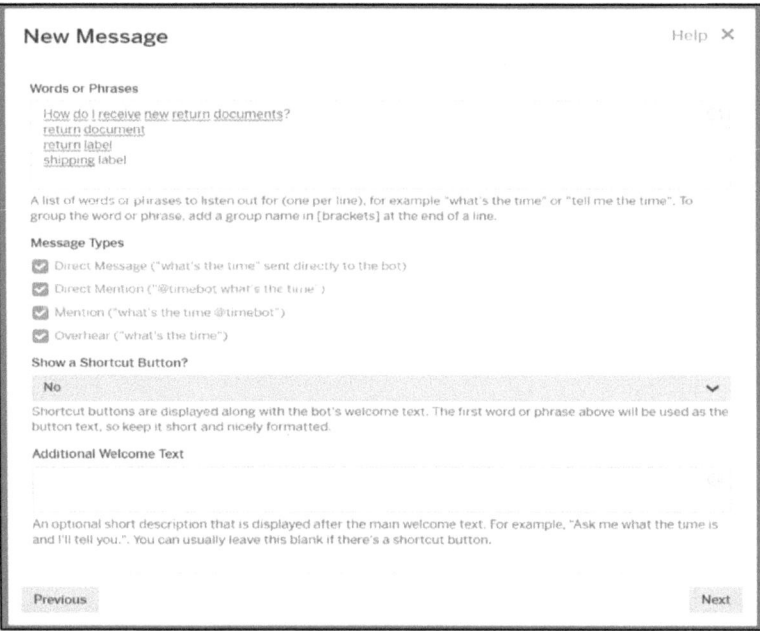

Figure 6: FlowXO 'New Message'

This is all the information required to set up a trigger. After the trigger is activated, the bot can ask a question. To set this up, one must click '+' to add a task. In the 'Choose a service' window, the action 'Ask a question' could be selected. The ask a question window has several options, such as question type (text or choice), question and validation for the answer:

Practical Use Case Analysis and Implementation

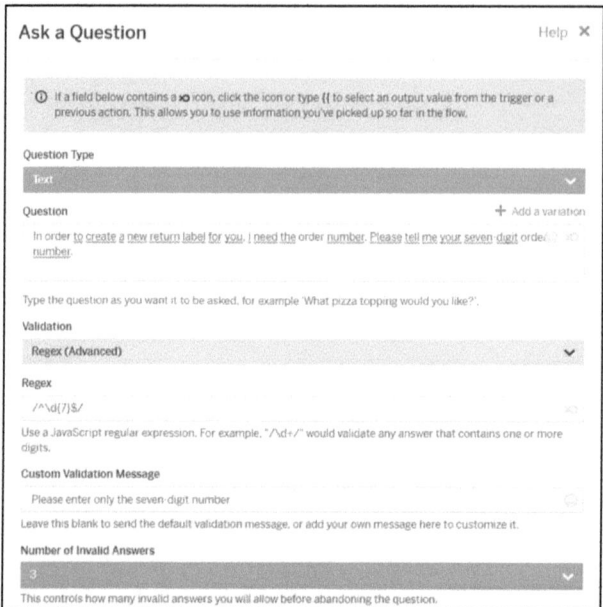

Figure 7: FlowXO 'Ask a Question'

If the validation of the question is successful and the user enters a seven-digit order number, it is possible to create an http request. A http request, for example 'https://www.shop.com/returns?order={{ask_a_question.parsed_answer}}', could prompt an online shop to check if the order is valid. FlowXO sets up the user's answer (a seven-digit number) automatically in the http request. The data output from the http request can be a link to download a return label or a negative answer from the online shop.

To answer the order number question in combination with the http request result, it is necessary to create another message with the link to download a return label:

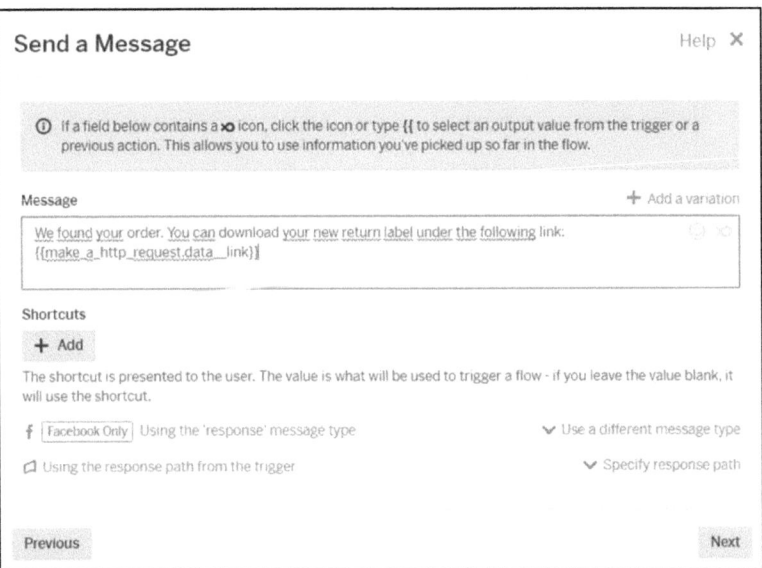

Figure 8: FlowXO 'Send a Message'

The answer should be only displayed if the http request responses with the link. This can be defined using a filter:

Practical Use Case Analysis and Implementation

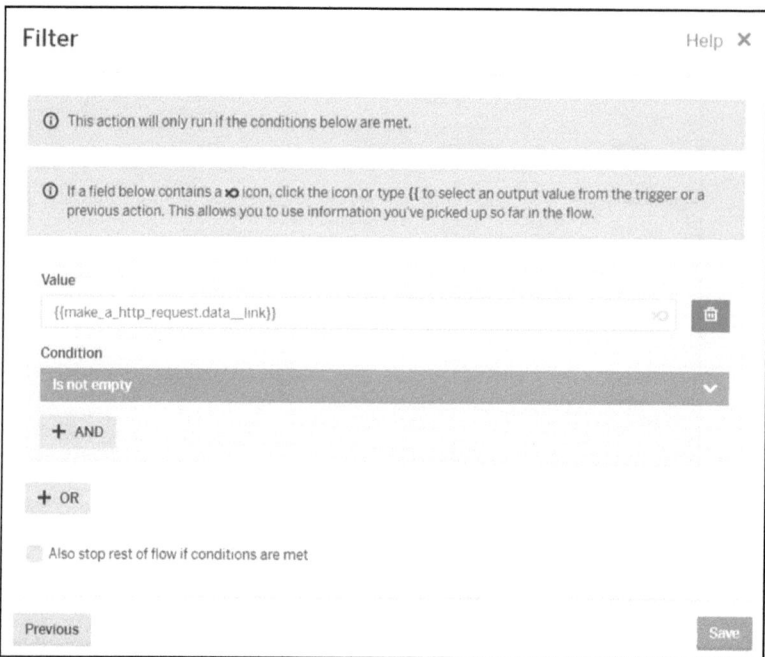

Figure 9: FlowXO 'Filter'

This allows the user to download a return label in the messenger. This can be tested directly in the test console:

Using this approach, a multitude of use cases can be implemented. In the example shown, only two answers were possible. Either there is an order, and therefore a return label, or not; however, various combinations, response options and triggers can be implemented. In addition to static answers, it is also possible to use real-time data from the online shop to display as many use cases as possible.

Practical Use Case Analysis and Implementation

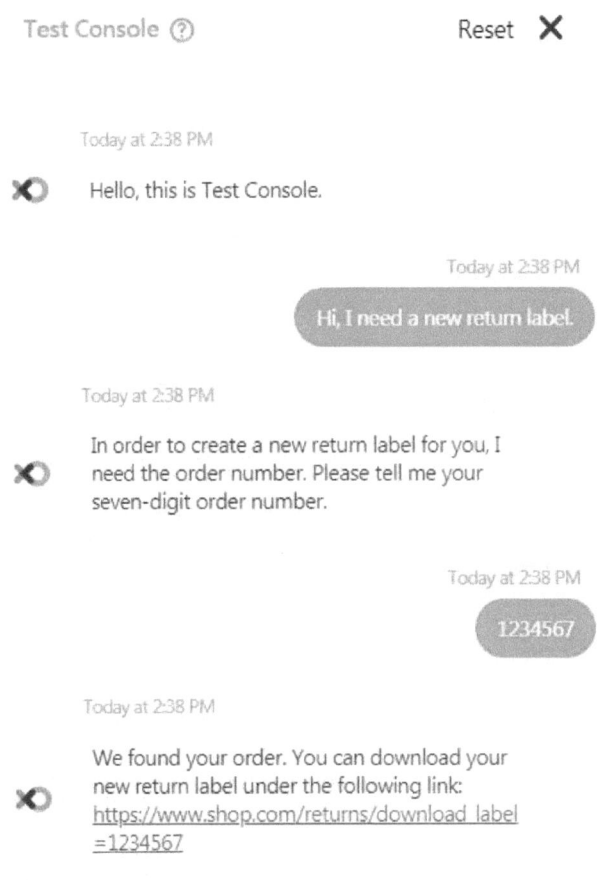

Figure 10: FlowXO 'Test Console'

4.4 Evaluation

FlowXO's service provides an easy process to get started with bot development. This becomes clear from the beginning. The tutorials and documentation make it possible to create a chatbot quickly and without much effort. Integration into platforms, such as Facebook, is also easy and does not require technical knowledge to implement. An automation of use cases is not planned, and all possible answers also have to be processed manually. There is, however, a large number of standardized use cases for e-commerce that can be mapped using FlowXO. The difficulty is therefore to capture correct use cases for day-to-day business and to map them cleanly. A meaningful database, which should be a core component of an e-commerce model anyway, is indispensable. In order not to give the end user the opportunity to ask ambiguous or unclear questions, it is important to direct the conversation and to communicate question options. In sum, it is possible to introduce a standardized chatbot with relatively little effort and cost.

5 Conclusion

Because of digitalization, automation processes are very important and interesting for companies. Especially chatbots, which can be classified in different ways, offer many possibilities. Both end users and operators use them for reasons of productivity and simplified communication. Positive politeness and short response times have a positive impact on perception by end users. In the context of e-commerce, chatbots can help customers prepare for a sale, assist them during the purchase phase and support them in the after-sale phase. The research conducted here shows that due to fast data processing during almost all phases of the purchase process in the chatbot and thus outside the online shop, for example on social media platforms such as Facebook, can be mapped. The extent to which dealers should use the system must be examined on a case-by-case basis. The application intervenes dramatically in the customer journey, resulting in the customer not getting an exact picture of the retailer on social media platforms. In this respect, it would be of interest for further research to analyze the use of chatbots and their effects on the customer journey. The hypothetical possibilities of chatbots show a clear advantage compared to the renunciation of chatbots. As long as a good implementation is provided, the advantage of real-time customer management should not be dismissed, and the cost advantage compared to a human customer service can significantly influence the success of an e-commerce model. Using additional information gleaned from conversations, a retailer can recommend individualized and tailor-made offers to the customer and generate added value resulting in additional income for both the customer and the retailer. There is a variety of methods for developing a chatbot. The present work focused on a look at a simplified design of a chatbot on the social media platform Facebook. With little effort and cost, even smaller dealers can quickly offer this service to their customers. The analysis would be interesting for the integration directly in the online shop to be able to influence the purchase process. In addition to tools shown by chatbot providers, which are suitable for use in standardized use cases, an overview of development frameworks, such as Microsoft Azure, Amazon Lex, Google Dialogflow and NLP engines, would be interesting in order to answer more complex questions. Certainly, the use of AI is a further indication of the superiority of chatbots over conventional collaborative live chats, which are only used during specific business hours and cannot process as much data. The customer experience must be taken into account in all considerations. The risk of incorrect address exists with the use of chatbots and should be considered thoroughly. Ultimately, the success of the deployment and use of chatbots depends on the fulfilment of expectations on the part of both the customer and the merchant. The present work has provided an overview of the chatbot landscape from an e-commerce perspective; however, it has also shown that there is still a number of questions and that the journey of the chatbots has only just begun.

Works Cited

Abraham, A. (2018). Emerging Technologies in Data Mining and Information Security (3rd ed.). Springer, 2012

Albach, H. (2002). Marketing-Management. Wiesbaden: Gabler, 2002

Bager, J. (2016). Gesprächige Automaten. Magazin für Computertechnik. 24, 2012

Bange, C., Schinzer, H. (2005). Rentablere Kundenbeziehungen durch automatisierte Analyse und Personalisierung. In: R. Thome, H. Schinzer & M. Hepp [ed.]: Electronic Commerce und Electronic Business - Mehrwert durch Integration und Automation. (pp. 53-79). München: Franz Vahlen, 2005

Baran, R. J., Galka, R. J. (2017). Customer relationship management: The foundation of contemporary marketing strategy (2nd ed.). New York: Routledge, 2017

Blythe, J. (2012). Essentials of marketing (5.th ed.). Harlow: Pearson, 2012

Braun, A. (2003). Chatbots in der Kundenkommunikation. Berlin: Springer, 2003

Brézillon, P., Gonzalez, A. J. (2014). Context in Computing: A Cross-Disciplinary Approach for Modeling the Real World. New York, Heidelberg, London: Springer, 2014

Broeckelmann, P. (2010). Konsumentenentscheidungen im Mobile Commerce : Eine empirische Untersuchung des Einflusses von mobilen Services auf das Kaufverhalten. Wiesbaden: Gabler Verlag / GWV Fachverlage GmbH, Wiesbaden, 2010

Bruhn, M. (2016). Marketing : Grundlagen für Studium und Praxis (13.th ed.). Wiesbaden: Springer Fachmedien Wiesbaden, 2016

Brugnoli, G. (2009, Februar 23): Connecting the dots of user experience. Retrieved from http://de.slideshare.net/frogdesign/brugnoli-system-ux-1061731.

Buschmann, M. (2003). Strategien für Dialogführungssysteme - Automation der Kundenkommunikation im Kontaktkanal Internet. In: C. Lindner [ed.]: Avatare - Digitale Sprecher für Business und Marketing. (pp. 95-109). Berlin Heidelberg: Springer-Verlag, 2003

Buttle, F. (2009). Customer relationship management : Concepts and technologies (2nd ed.). Amsterdam: Elsevier Butterworth-Heinemann, 2009

Buxmann, P., Schmidt, H. (2018). Künstliche Intelligenz : Mit Algorithmen zum wirtschaftlichen Erfolg. Berlin, Heidelberg: Springer Berlin Heidelberg, 2018

Ceyp, M., Scupin, J. (2013). Erfolgreiches Social Media Marketing : Konzepte, Maßnahmen und Praxisbeispiele. Wiesbaden: Springer Fachmedien Wiesbaden, 2013

Chaffey, D. (2001). Internet-Marketing. München: Pearson Studium, 2001

Court, D., Elzinga, D., Mulder, S., Vetvik, O. J. (2009, June): The consumer decision journey. Retrieved from http://www.mckinsey.com/insights/marketing_sales/the_consumer_decision_journey.

Crivelli, G. (2016). Warum Chatbots die neuen Apps sind. Netzwoche. Retrieved from http://www.netzwoche.ch/storys/2016-10-04/warum-chatbots-die-neuen-appssind.

Dahlén, M., Lange, F., & Smith, T. (2010). Marketing communications : A brand narrative approach. Chichester, West Sussex: Wiley, 2010

Dale, R. (2016). The return of the chatbots. In: Kompatsiaris, I., Cave, J., Satsiou, A., Carle, G., Passani, A., Kontopoulos, E., Diplaris, S., McMillan, D. (2017). Internet Science: 4th International Conference, INSCI 2017, Thessaloniki, Greece, November 22-24, 2017, Proceedings (pp. 811 - 817) Springer, 2017

Dallmer, H. (2002). Das Handbuch Direct-Marketing & more (8.th ed.). Wiesbaden: Gabler, 2002

Dreyer, A., Dehner, C. (2003): Kundenzufriedenheit im Tourismus. Entstehung, Messung und Sicherung mit Beispielen aus der Hotelbranche. (2nd ed.). München, 2003

Dubberly, H., Evenson, S. (2008, May 1). The Experience Cycle. Retrieved from http://www.dubberly.com/articles/interactions-the-experience-cycle.html.

Ebersbach, A., Glaser, M., & Heigl, R.. (2016). Social Web (3rd ed.). Konstanz: UVK Verlagsgesellschaft GmbH, 2016

Eicher, D. (2016, November 16). Chatbots. Retrieved from http://www.digitalwiki.de/chatbots.

Ertel, W. (2017). Introduction to Artificial Intelligence. Springer, 2017

Esch, F.-R., Gawlowski, D., Rühl, V. (2012). Erlebnisorientierte Kommunikation sinnvoll gestalten und managen. In: Bauer, H., Heinrich, D., Samak, M. [ed.]: Erlebniskommunikation. Erfolgsfaktoren für die Marketingpraxis. (pp. 13-30) Berlin: Springer, 2012

Esch, F.-R., Herrmann, A., Sattler, H. (2017). Marketing : Eine managementorientierte Einführung (5.th ed.). München: Verlag Franz Vahlen, 2017

Fill, C. (2001). Marketing-Kommunikation : Konzepte und Strategien (2nd ed.). München: Pearson Studium, 2001

Fill, C., Turnbull, S. (2016). Marketing communications : Discovery, creation and conversations (7.th ed.). Harlow, England: Pearson, 2016

Franke, M., Schulz, C. (2016). Smarter Service - Wie smart ist der digitale Kundenservice heute eigentlich? In: M. Gouthier [ed.]: Kundenbindung durch kosteneffiziente Service Excellence. (pp. 91-105). Baden-Baden: Nomos Verlagsgesellschaft, 2016

Gabriel, R., Röhrs, H. (2017). Social Media : Potenziale, Trends, Chancen und Risiken. Berlin, Heidelberg: Springer Berlin Heidelberg, 2017

Gast, O. (2018). User Experience im E-Commerce : Messung von Emotionen bei der Nutzung interaktiver Anwendungen. Wiesbaden: Springer Fachmedien Wiesbaden, 2018

Goksel Canbek, N., Mutlu, M. E. (2016). On the track of Artificial Intelligence: Learning with intelligent personal assistants. Journal of Human Sciences 13, 1 (2016), (pp. 592–601)

Hauk, J., Schulz, C. (2012). Customer Experience Management für Telekommunikationsunternehmen. In: Bruhn, M., Hadwich, K. [ed.] (2012). Customer Experience : Forum Dienstleistungsmanagement. (pp. 385-406) Wiesbaden: Gabler Verlag, 2012

Heinemann, G. (2018). Der neue Online-Handel : Geschäftsmodelle, Geschäftssysteme und Benchmarks im E-Commerce (9th ed.). Wiesbaden: Springer Fachmedien Wiesbaden, 2018

Herbstritt, K. (2015). Markenmanagement : Von der Unternehmensmarke zur Markenpersönlichkeit?. Hamburg: Diplomica Verlag GmbH. 2015

Heymann-Reder, D. (2011). Social-Media-Marketing : Erfolgreiche Strategien für Sie und Ihr Unternehmen. München: Addison-Wesley, 2011

Hildebrand, V. G. (2000). Kundenbindung mit Online Marketing. In: J. Link [ed.]: Wettbewerbsvorteile durch Online Marketing. (pp. 55-75). Berlin Heidelberg: Springer-Verlag, 2000

Hippner, H. (2011). Grundlagen des CRM : Strategie, Geschäftsprozesse und IT-Unterstützung (3rd. ed.). Wiesbaden: Gabler, 2011

Hoffmann, A. (2018). Chatbots: Einführung in die Zukunft von Marketing, PR und CRM. München: Franzis Verlag, 2018

Hoffman, D., Novak, T. (1998). A New Marketing Paradigm for Electronic Commerce. The Information Society. 13.

Holland, H. (2016). Dialogmarketing : Offline- und Online-Marketing, Mobile- und Social Media-Marketing (4.th ed.). München: Verlag Franz Vahlen, 2016

Holland, H., Ramanathan, N. (2016). Customer Experience Management. In: T. Schwarz [ed.]: Leitfaden Digitale Transormation - Beispiele aus der Praxis. (pp. 187-198). Waghäusel: marketing-BÖRSE GmbH, 2016

Homburg, C., Bruhn, M. (2006). Handbuch Kundenbindungsmanagement : Strategien und Instrumente für ein erfolgreiches CRM (9th ed.). Wiesbaden: Springer Gabler, 2006

Hougaard, S., & Bjerre, M. (2002). Strategic relationship marketing. Berlin: Springer, 2002

Ingram, T. N., LaForge, R. W., Avila, R. A., Schwepker, C. H., Williams, M. R. (2015). Sales management : Analysis and decision making (9th ed.). New York ; London: Routledge, 2015

Janarthanam, S. (2017). Hands-On Chatbots and Conversational UI Development: Build chatbots and voice user interfaces with Chatfuel, Dialogflow, Microsoft Bot Framework, Twilio, and Alexa Skills. Birmingham: Packt Publishing Ltd, 2017

Kamps, I., Schetter, D. (2018). Performance Marketing : Der Wegweiser zu einem mess- und steuerbaren Marketing – Einführung in Instrumente, Methoden und Technik. Wiesbaden: Springer Fachmedien Wiesbaden, 2018

Koch, M., Richter, A. (2009). Enterprise 2.0 : Planung, Einführung und erfolgreicher Einsatz von Social Software in Unternehmen (2nd ed.). München: Oldenbourg, 2009

Kollewe, T., Keukert, M. (2016). Praxiswissen E-Commerce (2nd ed.). Heidelberg: O'Reilly, 2016

Kotler, P., Bliemel, F., Keller, K. L. (2017). Marketing-Management : Analyse, Planung und Kontrolle. (15.th ed.). Stuttgart: Poeschel, 2017

Kotler, P. (2013). Principles of marketing (6.th European ed.). Harlow: Pearson, 2013

Krafft, M. [ed.], Mann, A. (2007). Direct-Marketing. Wiesbaden: Gabler, 2007

Kruse Brandão, T., Wolfram, G. (2018). Digital Connection : Die bessere Customer Journey mit smarten Technologien – Strategie und Praxisbeispiele. Wiesbaden: Springer Fachmedien Wiesbaden, 2018

Kumar, V., Reinartz, Werner. (2018). Customer relationship management : Concept, strategy, and tools (3rd. ed.). Berlin: Springer.

Langer, C. (2016). Kundenservice in Echtzeit mittels Live-Chat. In: Marketing Resultant GmbH [ed.]: Die digitale Zukunft des Kundenservice. (pp. 36-45). Retrieved from http://marketing-resultant.de/wp-content/uploads/Zukunft-Digitaler_Kundenservice_2016_eBook.pdf.

Leußer, W. (2011). Datenqualitätsmanagement Im Customer-Relationship-Management. Hamburg: Dr. Kovac Verlag, 2011

MacInnis, D. J., Price, L. L. (1987): The role of imagery in information processing. Review and extensions. In: Journal of Consumer Research 13, nr. 4, pp. 473-491.

Maes, P. (2018). Disruptive Selling: A New Strategic Approach to Sales, Marketing and Customer Service. London: Kogan Page Publishers, 2018

Manning, H., Bodine, K. (2012). Outside in: The Power of Putting Customers at the Center of Your Business. Boston: Houghton Mifflin Harcourt, 2012

McDaniel, C. D., Lamb, C. W., Hair, J. F. (2012). Marketing essentials (7. ed., international ed.). South Melbourne: South-Western Cengage Learning, 2012

McTear, M., Callejas, Z., Griol, D. (2016). The Conversational Interface: Talking to Smart Devices. Springer, 2016

Meffert, H., Burmann, C., Kirchgeorg, M. (2012). Marketing: Grundlagen marktorientierter Unternehmensführung Konzepte – Instrumente – Praxisbeispiele (12.th ed.). Wiesbaden: Springer Gabler, 2015

Meffert, H., Bruhn, M., Hadwich, Karsten. (2015). Dienstleistungsmarketing - Grundlagen, Konzepte, Methoden. 8. Auflage. Wiesbaden: Springer Fachmedien, 2015

Mengue Nkoa, C. (2006). Effiziente Gestaltung bankspezifischer CRM-Prozesse : Ein praxisorientiertes Referenz-Organisationsmodell. Wiesbaden: Deutscher Universitäts-Verlag / GWV Fachverlage GmbH, Wiesbaden, 2006

Möbus, et al. (2006). Web-Kommunikation mit OpenSource Chatbots, Virtuelle Messen, Rich-Media-Content. Berlin, Heidelberg: Springer-Verlag Berlin Heidelberg, 2006

Niegemann, H. M., Domagk, S., Hessel, S., Hein, A., Hupfer, M., Zobel, A. (2008) Kompendium multimediales Lernen. Berlin Heidelberg: Springer-Verlag, 2008

Nguyen, P., Pupillo, N. (2012). Branded Moments - Vom zufälligen Kundenerlebnis zur aktiven Gestaltung von Wow-Momenten in der Kundeninteraktion bei Vodafone Deutschland. In: Bruhn, M., Hadwich, K. [ed.] (2012). Customer experience. (pp. 317 - 330) Wiesbaden: Springer Gabler, 2012

Patwardhan, P., Ramaprasad, J. (2005) Rational Integrative Model of Online Consumer Decision Making, Journal of Interactive Advertising, 6:1, 2-13

Peppers, D., Rogers, M. (2016). Managing customer experience and relationships : A strategic framework (3rd ed.). Hoboken, New Jersey: John Wiley & Sons, 2016

Peter, J. P., Olson, J. C. (1999). Consumer behavior and marketing strategy (5th ed.). Boston: Irwin McGraw-Hill, 1999

Peterson, R., Balasubramanian, S., Bronnenberg, B. (1997). Exploring the Implications of the Internet for Consumer Marketing. Journal of the Academy of Marketing Science. 25. pp. 329-346.

Plassmann, E. (2011) Bibliotheken und Informationsgesellschaft in Deutschland : eine Einführung. (2nd ed.) Wiesbaden : Harrassowitz, 2011

Rajola, F. (2003). Customer Relationship Management: Organizational and Technological Perspectives. Heidelberg: Springer, 2003

Rashid, K., Das, A. (2017). Build Better Chatbots: A Complete Guide to Getting Started with Chatbots. Apress, 2017

Richardson, A. (2010, October 28). Understanding Customer Experience. Retrieved from http://blogs.hbr.org/2010/10/understanding-customer-experie/.

Runia, P., Wahl, F., Geyer, O., Thewißen, C. (2015). Marketing : Prozess- und praxisorientierte Grundlagen (4.th ed.). Berlin: De Gruyter Oldenbourg, 2015

Rutschmann, M. (2018). Kaufprozessorientiertes Marketing: Stop Branding, Start Selling! : Wie neueste Erkenntnisse aus der Verhaltensforschung und den Neurowissenschaften Marketing und Vertrieb beflügeln. Wiesbaden: Springer Fachmedien Wiesbaden, 2018

Saeed, K., Chaki, N., Pati, B., Bakshi, S., Mohapatra, D. (2018). Progress in Advanced Computing and Intelligent Engineering : Proceedings of ICACIE 2016, Volume 1. Singapore: Springer Singapore, 2016

Samuelsen, P. (2003). Die Bedeutung von natürlichsprachlichen Dialogsystemen in Internet-Business. In: C. Lindner [ed]: Avatare - Digitale Sprecher für Business und Marketing. (pp. 27-35). Berlin Heidelberg: Springer-Verlag, 2003

Schlicht, M. (2016, April 20). The Complete Beginner's Guide To Chatbots. Retrieved https://chatbotsmagazine.com/the-complete-beginner-s-guide-to-chatbots-8280b7b906ca.

Schubert, P., Selz, D. (2007). Measuring the effectiveness of e-commerce Web sites. In: Barnes, S. [ed]. (2007). E-commerce and v-business : Digital enterprise in the twenty-first century (2nd ed.). Amsterdam: Butterworth-Heinemann.. (pp. 83-102), 2007

Works Cited

Schmitt, B. H., Mangold, M. (2004): Kundenerlebnis als Wettbewerbsvorteil. Mit Customer Experience Management Marken und Märkte Gewinn bringend gestalten. Wiesbaden: Betriebswirtschaftlicher Verlag Dr. Th. Gabler/GWV Fachverlage GmbH, 2004

Schmitt, B. (2011). Experience marketing : Concepts, frameworks and consumer insights. Boston: Now, 2011

Schmitt, B., Rogers, D. (2008). Handbook on brand and experience management. Cheltenham, U.K.: Edward Elgar, 2008

Scott, D. M. (2014). Die neuen Marketing- und PR-Regeln im Social Web : Wie Sie mit Social Media und Content Marketing, Blogs, Pressemitteilungen und viralem Marketing Ihre Kunden erreichen (4.th ed.). Heidelberg: Mitp, 2014

Shaw, C., Ivens, J. (2002): Building great customer experiences. New York: Palgrave Macmillan, 2002

Smith, A., Rupp, W. (2003). Strategic online customer decision making: Leveraging the transformational power of the Internet. Online Information Review. 27. pp. 418-432.

Smolinski, R., Gerdes, M., Siejka, M., Bodek, M. (2017). Innovationen und Innovationsmanagement in der Finanzbranche. Wiesbaden: Springer Fachmedien Wiesbaden, 2017

Solomon, M. R. (2015). Consumer behavior : Buying, having, and being (11th ed., global ed.). Boston: Pearson, 2015

Stojek, M. (2000). Customer Relationship Management - Software, Strategie, Prozess oder Konzept? Die Fachzeitschrift für Information Management & Consulting, 15(1), pp. 37-42.

Stone, B., Jacobs, R. (2001). Successful direct marketing methods (7th ed.). Chicago, Ill.: McGraw-Hill, 2001

Stricker, A. (2003). Darf's ein bisschen menschlicher sein? - Virtuelle Charaktere am Point of Sale. In: C. Lindner [ed]: Avatare - Digitale Sprecher für Business und Marketing. (pp. 169-184). Berlin Heidelberg: Springer-Verlag, 2003

Sulaiman, A., Naqshbandi, M. M. (2014). Social media: Dynamism, issues, and challenges. Singapore: Partridge, 2014

Tyagi, C.L., Kumar A. (2001). Consumer Behaviour. New Delhi: Atlantic Publishers & Dist, 2004

Verspoor K., Cohen K.B. (2013) Natural Language Processing. In: Dubitzky W., Wolkenhauer O., Cho KH., Yokota H. [ed] Encyclopedia of Systems Biology. New York: Springer, 2013

Vogt, M. (2016, November 21). Wie Chatbots den Kundenservice revolutionieren wollen. Retrieved from https://www.ccw.eu/blog/wie-chatbots-den-kundenservice-revolutionieren-wollen/.

Weinberg, T. (2015). Social-Media-Marketing : Strategien für Twitter, Facebook & Co. (4th ed.). Beijing: O'Reilly, 2015

Wikström, S. (2008): A consumer perspective on experience creation. In: Journal of Consumer Behaviour Jg. 7, 1, pp. 31-50.

Wirtz, B. W. (2018). Electronic Business (6th ed.). Wiesbaden: Springer Gabler, 2018

Yi, Y. (2014). Customer value creation behavior. London: Routledge, 2014

Internet Sources

aspect.com: https://www.accenture.com/t00010101T000000_w_/br-pt/_acnmedia/PDF-45/Accenture-Chatbots-Customer-Service.pdf, 01.12.2018

analyticsinsight.net: https://www.analyticsinsight.net/top-7-chatbot-platforms-to-build-bots-for-your-business/, 23.11.2018

aspect.com: https://www.aspect.com/globalassets/2016-aspect-consumer-experience-indexsurvey_index-results-final.pdf, 01.12.2018

ccw.eu: https://www.ccw.eu/blog/kuenstliche-intelligenz-im-kundenservice/, 01.12.2018

ccw.eu: https://www.ccw.eu/blog/kuenstliche-intelligenz-und-robotics-wie-sie-chatbots-gewinnbringend-einsetzen/, 01.12.2018

chatbotslife.com: https://chatbotslife.com/to-use-chatbot-buttons-or-not-to-use-chatbot-buttons-745af3f0deec, 23.11.2018

chatbotslife.com: https://chatbotslife.com/to-use-chatbot-buttons-or-not-to-use-chatbot-buttons-745af3f0deec, 27.11.2018

Works Cited

chatbotslife.com: https://chatbotslife.com/chatbot-and-product-recommender-a-great-combo-ab35beb1bacd, 29.11.2018

chatbotslife.com: https://chatbotslife.com/10-ai-bots-with-human-names-7efd7047be34, 03.12.2018

chatbotsjournal.com: https://chatbotsjournal.com/25-chatbot-platforms-a-comparative-table-aeefc932eaff, 23.11.2018

chatbotsmagazine.com: https://chatbotsmagazine.com/worlds-biggest-ai-engines-comparison-46e421413ab, 01.11.2018

chatbotsmagazine.com: https://chatbotsmagazine.com/what-it-takes-to-build-enterprise-class-chatbots-db62227013c0, 23.11.2018

chatbotsmagazine.com: https://chatbotsmagazine.com/chatbots-stage-i-ecommerce-checkout-f6920899ce0d, 27.11.2018

chatfuel.com: https://chatfuel.com/pricing.html, 23.11.2018

computerworld.com: https://www.computerworld.com.au/article/602764/transforming-customer-experience-chatbots/, 30.11.2018

deloitte.com: https://www2.deloitte.com/content/dam/Deloitte/in/Documents/strategy/in-strategy-innovation-conversational-chatbots-lets-chat-final-report-noexp.pdf, 23.11.2018

deloitte.com: https://www2.deloitte.com/content/dam/Deloitte/ru/Documents/financial-services/artificial-intelligence-in-insurance.pdf, 30.11.2018

ecommerce-chatbots.com: http://ecommerce-chatbots.com/best-buy-order-status-chatbot/, 23.11.2018

ey.com: https://consulting.ey.com/chatbots-engaging-with-your-customers-like-a-friend/, 29.11.2018

fittkaumaass.de: http://www.fittkaumaass.de/news/chatbots-von-jedem-zweiten-online-kaeufer-abgelehnt, 01.12.2018

forbes.com: https://www.forbes.com/sites/bernardmarr/2018/05/18/how-artificial-intelligence-is-making-chatbots-better-for-businesses/#4757d4eb4e72, 23.11.2018

Works Cited

forbes.com: https://www.forbes.com/sites/stevendennis/2017/08/31/unsustainable-customer-acquisition-costs-make-much-of-ecommerce-profit-proof/#3597a4203e77, 01.12.2018

futurecom.ch: https://www.futurecom.ch/angebot/e-commerce/futurecom-e-commerce-studie/?gclid=CIjV75W4q9MCFVTNGwodqFwAZw, 30.11.2018

flowxo.com: https://flowxo.com/pricing/, 23.11.2018

geekflare.com: https://geekflare.com/chatbot-development-frameworks/, 23.11.2018

ibm.com: https://www.ibm.com/blogs/watson/2017/10/how-chatbots-reduce-customer-service-costs-by-30-percent/, 01.12.2018

inc.com: https://www.inc.com/john-brandon/the-day-is-coming-when-customer-service-will-be-run-by-chatbots.html, 19.12.2018

jekelteam.de: https://www.jekelteam.de/wie-koennen-chatbots-den-kundenservice-revolutionieren, 01.12.2018

magronet.de: http://www.magronet.de/messenger-chatbots-zukunft-kommunikation/, 30.11.2018

medium.com: https://medium.com/makerobos/what-are-contextual-chatbots-how-they-can-make-a-world-of-difference-in-user-experience-e7446c96664e, 01.11.2018

medium.com: https://medium.com/janis/how-to-take-over-your-chatfuel-bot-without-leaving-slack-177ffabd4cfd, 13.11.2018

medium.com: https://medium.com/read-it-quik/building-a-chatbot-platform-a-cautious-approach-786f5b29b074, 23.11.2018

statista.com: https://www.statista.com/statistics/417295/facebook-messenger-monthly-active-users/, 29.11.2018

statista.com: https://de.statista.com/statistik/studie/id/41378/dokument/conversational-commerce-statista-dossier/, 30.11.2018

statista.com: https://de.statista.com/statistik/studie/id/41378/dokument/conversational-commerce-statista-dossier/, 01.12.2018

Works Cited

statista.com: https://de.statista.com/statistik/daten/studie/222135/umfrage/taeglich-aktive-facebook-nutzer-weltweit/, 03.12.2018

statsbot.co: https://blog.statsbot.co/chatbots-machine-learning-e83698b1a91e, 03.12.2018

techcrunch.com: https://techcrunch.com/2016/07/01/shatbots/?guccounter=1, 23.11.2018

theguardian.com: https://www.theguardian.com/technology/2018/nov/18/how-can-you-tell-who-is-human-online-chatbots, 23.11.2018

thenextweb.com: https://thenextweb.com/contributors/2018/06/03/1128084/, 23.11.2018

wired.com: https://www.wired.com/story/replika-open-source/, 29.11.2018